NOETIC SCRYING: DIVINING THROUGH COGNITIVE STATES

Mindfulness and Meditation
as Divinatory Tools

D.R. T STEPHENS

S.D.N Publishing

Copyright © 2023 S.D.N Publishing

All rights reserved

The characters and events portrayed in this book are fictitious. Any similarity to real persons, living or dead, is coincidental and not intended by the author.

No part of this book may be reproduced, or stored in a retrieval system, or transmitted in any form or by any means, electronic, mechanical, photocopying, recording, or otherwise, without express written permission of the publisher.

ISBN: 9798866529018

CONTENTS

Title Page
Copyright
General Disclaimer — 1
Chapter 1: A Friendly Introduction to Noetic Scrying — 4
Chapter 2: Mindfulness: The Basics — 7
Chapter 3: Origins of Meditation — 9
Chapter 4: A Spectrum of Cognitive States — 12
Chapter 5: Mindfulness Techniques for Beginners — 16
Chapter 6: The Anatomy of Meditation — 19
Chapter 7: The Role of Breath in Mindfulness — 22
Chapter 8: Sensory Awareness and Perception — 25
Chapter 9: Mindfulness and Emotions — 28
Chapter 10: The Body-Scan Method — 32
Chapter 11: Simple Meditation Rituals — 36
Chapter 12: Observing Thought Patterns — 39
Chapter 13: Mindful Eating and Consumption — 42
Chapter 14: Yoga and Physical Mindfulness — 45
Chapter 15: Zen and the Art of Presence — 48
Chapter 16: Metacognition: Thinking About Thinking — 51
Chapter 17: Mindfulness and Neural Plasticity — 54
Chapter 17 invites readers on a journey through the — 57

...ds, illumina... ...tation Explored	60
Chapter 18: Transcend... ...indfulness	63
Chapter 19: Biofeed...ased Stress Reduction (MBSR)	66
Chapter 20: Mindf... ...our Meditation Practices	69
Chapter 21: De...ness and Quantum Thinking	73
Chapter 22: M...fulness and Creativity	77
Chapter 23... ...aoist Meditation Techniques	80
Chapter ... Vipassana Meditation	83
Chapter...5: Vipassana Meditation	83
Chapter...6: The Psychology of Mindfulness	86
Chapter 27: Self-Compassion in Mindfulness	89
Chapter 28: Theravada Meditation Practices	92
Chapter 29: Cognitive Dissonance and Mindfulness	95
Chapter 30: Mindfulness in Daily Routines	98
Chapter 31: Mindfulness and Social Relationships	101
Chapter 32: Dream Yoga and Lucid Dreaming	104
Chapter 33: Esoteric Traditions in Mindfulness	107
Chapter 34: Mindfulness and Non-Dual Awareness	111
Chapter 35: Advanced Sensory Perception Techniques	114
Chapter 36: Kundalini and Energy Work	117
Chapter 37: Consciousness Altering Substances and Mindfulness	120
Chapter 38: Mindfulness and Meta-Ethics	123
Chapter 39: Quantum Consciousness and Mindfulness	127
Chapter 40: The Shadow Self and Mindfulness	130
Chapter 41: Mindfulness and the Multiverse	133
Chapter 42: Advanced Mind-Mapping Techniques	136
Chapter 43: Mindfulness and Cosmic Unity	139

Chapter 44: Noetic Scrying in Mystical Traditions	142
Chapter 45: Mindfulness in Virtual Reality	145
Chapter 46: Existentialism and Mindfulness	149
Chapter 47: Mindfulness and Epigenetics	152
Chapter 48: A Friendly, Positive Conclusion	156
THE END	159

GENERAL DISCLAIMER

This book is intended to provide informative and educational material on the subject matter covered. The author(s), publisher, and any affiliated parties make no representations or warranties with respect to the accuracy, applicability, completeness, or suitability of the contents herein and specifically disclaim any implied warranties of merchantability or fitness for a particular purpose.

The information contained in this book is for general information purposes only and is not intended to serve as legal, medical, financial, or any other form of professional advice. Readers should consult with appropriate professionals before making any decisions based on the information provided. Neither the author(s) nor the publisher shall be held responsible or liable for any loss, damage, injury, claim, or otherwise, whether direct or indirect, consequential, or incidental, that may occur as a result of applying or misinterpreting the information in this book.

This book may contain references to third-party websites, products, or services. Such references do not constitute an endorsement or recommendation, and the author(s) and publisher are not responsible for any outcomes related to these third-party references.

In no event shall the author(s), publisher, or any affiliated parties be liable for any direct, indirect, punitive, special, incidental, or other consequential damages arising directly or indirectly from any use of this material, which is provided "as is," and without warranties of any kind, express or implied.

By reading this book, you acknowledge and agree that you assume all risks and responsibilities concerning the applicability and consequences of the information provided. You also agree to indemnify, defend, and hold harmless the author(s), publisher, and any affiliated parties from any and all liabilities, claims, demands, actions, and causes of action whatsoever, whether or not foreseeable, that may arise from using or misusing the information contained in this book.

NOETIC SCRYING: DIVINING THROUGH COGNITIVE STATES

Although every effort has been made to ensure the accuracy of the information in this book as of the date of publication, the landscape of the subject matter covered is continuously evolving. Therefore, the author(s) and publisher expressly disclaim responsibility for any errors or omissions and reserve the right to update, alter, or revise the content without prior notice.

By continuing to read this book, you agree to be bound by the terms and conditions stated in this disclaimer. If you do not agree with these terms, it is your responsibility to discontinue use of this book immediately.

CHAPTER 1: A FRIENDLY INTRODUCTION TO NOETIC SCRYING

Welcome, curious mind, to the fascinating journey of "Noetic Scrying: Divining Through Cognitive States." As you turn these pages, you embark on a path of exploration, not just of concepts and practices, but of your own mind and consciousness. This initial chapter serves as your gateway into the realm where mindfulness and meditation intertwine with the ancient art of divination, offering a friendly primer to what lies ahead.

Understanding Noetic Scrying

Noetic scrying, at its core, is about exploring the vast landscapes of our inner selves. The term 'noetic' comes from the Greek word 'noēsis/noētikos,' meaning inner wisdom or direct knowing. Scrying, on the other hand, is a practice often associated with divination or the attempt to gain insight into a question or situation. It traditionally involves gazing into a medium, such as a crystal ball, to perceive significant symbols or visions. When these concepts blend, noetic scrying becomes a process of introspection and reflection through which one can attain profound personal insights and revelations, not by looking outward, but by delving deep into the cognitive states that shape our very being.

The Landscape of Cognitive States

Imagine your mind as a dynamic, ever-changing ecosystem. Here, cognitive states are akin to the various weathers and climates that influence this landscape. Some days, your mind might be a clear, tranquil lake, reflecting the serenity of mindfulness. On others, it might resemble a storm, with thoughts thundering and emotions flashing like lightning. These states range from the everyday waking consciousness to the deep tranquility of meditative states, each holding unique insights like hidden treasures waiting to be unearthed. As we traverse through this book, we'll learn to navigate and harness these states, transforming them into a divinatory tool for personal growth and understanding.

The Role of Mindfulness and Meditation

Mindfulness and meditation are the compass and map for our journey of noetic scrying. Mindfulness teaches us to anchor ourselves in the present moment, to observe our thoughts, emotions, and sensations without judgment. Meditation, on the other hand, guides us deeper, inviting us to explore the silent spaces between thoughts, to connect with a part of ourselves that is unswayed by the tumult of daily life. Together, they form a potent framework for self-exploration and divination, helping us to decode the messages whispered by our innermost selves.

In this exploration, we'll discover how mindfulness can be as simple as conscious breathing and as profound as a sustained meditation practice. We'll learn to observe the interplay of thoughts and emotions, to listen to the wisdom of our bodies, and to embrace the transformative power of stillness. As we advance through the chapters, the practices will deepen, the concepts will expand, and our understanding of noetic scrying will evolve, revealing its true potential as a tool for insight and transformation.

Embarking on the Journey

As you stand at the threshold of this adventure, remember that noetic scrying is not just a practice but a journey of self-discovery. It's about finding the oracle within, the part of you that knows beyond words and sees beyond appearances. Whether you're new to the concepts of mindfulness and meditation or an experienced practitioner, this book is designed to guide you step by step, from the basics to the most profound aspects of cognitive exploration.

So take a deep breath, set your intentions, and prepare to delve into the mysteries of your mind. Embrace the spirit of curiosity, and let it lead you through the pages ahead. With each chapter, you're not just learning; you're embarking on a personal voyage to the frontiers of your consciousness, where every insight is a revelation, and every moment of stillness is a divination. Welcome to "Noetic Scrying: Divining Through Cognitive States." Your journey begins now.

CHAPTER 2: MINDFULNESS: THE BASICS

Mindfulness, in its most distilled essence, is the art and science of being vividly present in the moment. It is a conscious awareness of our thoughts, feelings, bodily sensations, and surrounding environment with an attitude of openness and curiosity. This chapter serves as an introductory portal into the world of mindfulness, delineating its core principles and underscoring its significance in our daily lives.

The Foundation of Mindfulness

At its core, mindfulness is rooted in the simple act of paying attention. It's about noticing the details of our experiences as they unfold, without filtering them through the lens of judgment or preconceived notions. This may sound trivial, but in a world brimming with distractions and a human mind prone to wander, maintaining this kind of focused awareness can be remarkably challenging. The practice of mindfulness brings us back to the anchor of the present moment, which is where life happens.

Significance in Contemporary Life

The pertinence of mindfulness in contemporary life cannot be overstated. In an epoch characterized by relentless haste, digital inundation, and societal pressures, our minds can become entangled in a web of ceaseless thought and worry. This can lead to an array of adverse mental states such as stress, anxiety, and depression. Mindfulness introduces a pause, a breath of clarity, allowing us to step back from the tumult and observe our mental processes. By doing so, we foster a space of responsiveness rather than reactivity, enabling us to navigate the complexities of life with a steadier hand and a clearer mind.

Mindfulness in Action

The practice of mindfulness can permeate all facets of our existence. It's not confined to the cushion of meditation but extends to the most mundane activities like washing dishes, taking a walk, or even engaging in conversation. Mindfulness is about being fully engaged in the activity at hand, noticing the subtleties of each action, the sensations it elicits, and the thoughts and emotions it stirs. This quality of attention enriches our experiences, making even the ordinary seem luminous with details previously unnoticed.

In conclusion, mindfulness is a foundational skill that acts as a bedrock for the journey through noetic scrying and the exploration of cognitive states. It's not an esoteric art reserved for the few but a universal practice accessible to all. As we delve deeper into the subsequent chapters, the principles and practices of mindfulness will serve as the thread weaving through the tapestry of cognitive exploration, enhancing our understanding of the mind and its profound capabilities.

CHAPTER 3: ORIGINS OF MEDITATION

In our journey through the tapestry of noetic scrying and the cognitive states that serve as its substrate, it is crucial to delve into the ancient roots from which the practice of meditation springs. The origins of meditation are as rich and diverse as the cultures that nurtured them, yet they converge in a common quest: the pursuit of inner harmony and an elevated understanding of the self and the universe.

Ancient Lineages of Stillness

The seeds of meditation were sown in the fertile grounds of antiquity. Its tendrils can be traced back to the Vedas, ancient Indian scriptures, where the term "dhyana" signified deep contemplation. However, the Indian subcontinent was not the only cradle of meditation. Simultaneously, in the distant lands of China, Daoist sages sought harmony with the Tao through quietude and introspection. Meanwhile, in the heart of Africa, the indigenous tribes engaged in trance-inducing dances and rituals that bore a striking resemblance to meditative states.

In these disparate cultures, meditation was not merely a practice but a profound engagement with the metaphysical realms. It was seen as a bridge to the divine, a means to transcend the mundane and glimpse the ineffable truths of existence.

Diverse Traditions: A Tapestry of Techniques

As civilizations evolved, so did their meditative practices. In Buddhism, meditation became the cornerstone for achieving enlightenment, or Nirvana. The Buddha himself, after a profound experience under the Bodhi tree, espoused meditation as the path to awakening. In the Buddhist tradition, meditation encompasses a variety of practices, from mindfulness (Sati) to loving-kindness (Metta), each with its unique flavor and transformative potential.

Parallel to this, in the Judaic mystical tradition of Kabbalah, meditation served as a conduit to understand the nature of God and the cosmos. The Kabbalists, through contemplation and the recitation of sacred texts, sought to ascend the spiritual spheres and achieve a mystical union with the divine.

The Christian mystics, too, embraced meditation, though it often donned the cloak of prayer and contemplation. Saints like Teresa of Avila and John of the Cross described states of rapturous union with God, achieved through deep meditative prayer.

Cultural Syncretism and the Evolution of Meditation

As trade routes opened and civilizations intermingled, so did their spiritual practices. Meditation underwent a cultural syncretism, absorbing elements from various traditions and evolving into new forms. The Islamic practice of Sufism, for example, incorporated elements of Christian mysticism and Indian spirituality, resulting in a rich tapestry of meditative practices like Dhikr, where the repetition of divine names induces a state of spiritual ecstasy.

In the far East, the synthesis of Buddhism and the native Shinto beliefs gave rise to Zen, a tradition that emphasizes the direct experience of enlightenment through Zazen, a form of seated meditation. Zen's simplicity and focus on direct experience resonated deeply, influencing not just spiritual seekers but artists and warriors alike.

The Scientific Reawakening

The journey of meditation, from ancient scriptures to contemporary practices, has been both spiritual and secular. In recent decades, the scientific community has taken a keen interest in meditation, subjecting it to rigorous scrutiny. The findings have been illuminating, revealing the profound impact of meditation on mental health, cognitive function, and overall well-being. This scientific reawakening has demystified meditation, making it more accessible and integrating it into therapeutic modalities.

Concluding Reflections

The origins of meditation are a mosaic of human inquiry into the nature of existence. From the rishis of India to the monks of the Far East, and from the shamans of Africa to the mystics of the Abrahamic faiths, meditation has been a unifying thread in the human quest for understanding. It is this rich historical tapestry that lays the foundation for the contemporary practices of mindfulness and meditation as tools for divination through cognitive states.

As we continue our exploration in the subsequent chapters, let us carry with us the reverence for the profound legacy of meditation, recognizing its potential not just as a method for inner tranquility but as a means of divining the deeper truths of our existence.

CHAPTER 4: A SPECTRUM OF COGNITIVE STATES

Embarking on the voyage through the labyrinthine domains of the mind, we encounter a plethora of cognitive states, each with its distinctive features and idiosyncrasies. The spectrum of cognitive states encompasses a broad range of mental experiences, from the mundane to the mystical, from heightened alertness to profound tranquility. Understanding this spectrum is essential for anyone seeking to navigate the nuanced terrains of mindfulness and meditation. In this chapter, we delve into the classification and comprehension of various cognitive states, laying a foundational understanding for the mindfulness journey.

The Tapestry of Consciousness

Consciousness, a concept as elusive as it is fundamental, presents itself as a rich tapestry woven from the threads of our cognitive states. At one end of the spectrum lies our default state, the ordinary waking consciousness characterized by a sense of self, a continuous stream of thoughts, and a perception of the external world through our sensory organs. This is the cognitive state most familiar to us, the backdrop against which our daily lives unfold.

Transitioning along the spectrum, we encounter altered states of consciousness, realms that differ significantly from our everyday experiences. These altered states can be induced through various means, including meditation, deep contemplation, intense physical activity, or even through certain psychoactive substances. In these states, our perception of time, space, and self may warp, offering us glimpses into the profound depths of our psyche.

States of Meditation

The practice of meditation, a cornerstone of mindfulness, is intricately linked to the exploration of cognitive states. Meditation can be seen as a structured approach to altering consciousness, guiding practitioners through various states ranging from focused attention to deep absorption.

In focused attention meditation, practitioners concentrate on a singular object or thought, often encountering a state of heightened alertness and clarity. As one progresses, this may transition into a state of open monitoring, where awareness becomes panoramic, and one becomes a passive observer of all thoughts, sensations, and emotions.

At the deeper end of the meditative spectrum, one might experience states of flow or absorption, where the sense of individual self dissipates, and a feeling of unity with the object of meditation emerges. These states are often described as profoundly tranquil and imbued with a sense of ineffable insight.

The Unconscious Mind

The spectrum of cognitive states extends into the realms of the unconscious mind, a vast and largely uncharted territory. While our conscious mind navigates the world through logic and sensory inputs, the unconscious operates silently in the background, influencing our thoughts, feelings, and behaviors in ways that often elude our awareness.

Dreams, those enigmatic narratives that unfold in our sleep, are perhaps the most direct glimpse we have into our unconscious mind. Dream states, with their peculiar logic and symbolic imagery, provide fertile ground for self-exploration and insight, serving as a bridge between our conscious and unconscious selves.

The Transcendent and the Mystical

At the farthest reaches of the cognitive spectrum lie transcendent and mystical states, experiences that defy conventional explanation and challenge our understanding of reality. These states, often encountered by seasoned meditators, mystics, or under the influence of entheogens, are characterized by a profound sense of unity with the cosmos, a dissolution of the ego, and an encounter with the sacred or the divine.

Such experiences, though rare and elusive, have been reported across cultures and epochs, suggesting a universal aspect of human consciousness that transcends the boundaries of the ordinary mind.

Conclusion

The spectrum of cognitive states is as diverse as it is fascinating, offering a kaleidoscopic view of the human mind. By understanding and exploring this spectrum, we equip ourselves with a map for the inner journey, allowing us to navigate the varied terrains of consciousness with greater awareness and insight. As we progress through our exploration of mindfulness and meditation, this understanding becomes an indispensable guide, illuminating the path toward deeper self-knowledge and spiritual growth.

CHAPTER 5: MINDFULNESS TECHNIQUES FOR BEGINNERS

Mindfulness, a practice rooted in ancient traditions, has surged in popularity in the modern world as a remedy to the relentless pace and complexity of contemporary life. This chapter is dedicated to equipping novices with fundamental techniques of mindfulness, providing a scaffold upon which a more resilient and attentive state of being can be constructed. These techniques serve as a gateway to cultivating an enhanced awareness of the present moment, allowing individuals to engage with their immediate experience without judgment or distraction.

Foundational Practices

Embarking on the journey of mindfulness, one begins with the foundational practices, those that are integral to understanding and experiencing mindfulness in its purest form. Among these, 'Focused Attention' is paramount. This practice involves the deliberate concentration of one's attention on a single point of reference, such as the breath, a specific sensation, or an object. This not only anchors the mind in the present but also trains it to return to the focal point whenever it wanders.

Another fundamental technique is 'Open Monitoring'. In contrast to focused attention, open monitoring entails the broadening of one's awareness to encompass all aspects of experience without attachment or preference. Here, one observes thoughts, feelings, and sensations as they arise and pass, fostering a stance of detached observation.

Integration into Daily Life

One of the remarkable facets of mindfulness is its adaptability and relevance to everyday activities. 'Mindful Walking' is a practice that embodies this integration. By concentrating on the rhythm of one's steps, the sensation of the ground underfoot, and the surrounding sights and sounds, walking becomes an act of meditation. Similarly, 'Mindful Eating' encourages the savoring of each bite, attentiveness to flavors, textures, and the process of nourishment, transforming a routine activity into a mindful experience.

These practices do not demand extra time from one's schedule but rather a shift in perspective, imbuing mundane activities with a sense of presence and attentiveness.

Overcoming Challenges

Beginners often encounter hurdles in their mindfulness practice, such as restlessness, distraction, or frustration. It is crucial to approach these challenges with kindness and patience. Techniques such as 'Labeling Thoughts' can be particularly beneficial. When the mind wanders, one gently acknowledges it by mentally noting what type of thought has arisen before returning to the practice. This not only diminishes the disruptive power of distractions but also fosters a deeper understanding of one's mental patterns.

Another effective method is the use of 'Mindfulness Reminders'. These can be simple cues placed in one's environment or daily routine that prompt a moment of mindfulness. It could be as straightforward as pausing for a deep breath each time one opens a door or taking a moment of silence before beginning a meal.

In summary, mindfulness practices for beginners serve as essential building blocks in cultivating a mindful existence. These techniques, rooted in simplicity and accessibility, provide a foundation for greater awareness and presence in one's life. As practitioners grow in their practice, they can explore more nuanced and complex techniques, but the core principles learned at this stage remain a touchstone throughout their mindfulness journey.

CHAPTER 6: THE ANATOMY OF MEDITATION

Embarking on a journey of meditation is akin to delving into the architecture of your own mind, each practice revealing more layers and intricacies. This chapter serves as a foundational exploration into the various forms of meditation, providing a rudimentary understanding of their structures, intentions, and outcomes. Through this knowledge, practitioners can make informed choices about which methods resonate most profoundly with their individual quests for mindfulness and insight.

Diversity in Stillness: Understanding Different Meditation Forms

Meditation, despite being a universal term, encompasses a diverse array of practices, each with its own unique characteristics. Some techniques prioritize the cultivation of a laser-focused attention, known as concentrative meditation. This form often involves fixating one's awareness on a single point, be it the breath, a mantra, or even an external object, with the intention of honing mental discipline.

In contrast, mindfulness or insight meditation encourages a broad awareness of all aspects of experience. Practitioners of this form are akin to impartial observers, noting thoughts, sensations, and emotions without attachment or judgment, thus fostering a deeper understanding of the transient nature of reality.

Loving-kindness meditation, or Metta Bhavana, takes a different approach. It centers on the cultivation of unconditional love and compassion towards oneself and others, promoting an attitude of benevolence and empathy in daily life.

Another intriguing variant is walking meditation, which integrates movement with mindful awareness. Practitioners focus on the sensations and rhythm of walking, transforming a simple activity into a profound exercise in presence and mindfulness.

Embarking on the Path: Getting Started with Meditation

For beginners, the prospect of meditation can seem daunting. Yet, it is crucial to understand that meditation is less about achieving a specific state and more about the journey towards self-awareness and tranquility. It is a gradual process, and like learning any new skill, it requires patience and perseverance.

Initiating this practice can be as simple as setting aside a few minutes each day to sit in silence, focusing on the breath. As one becomes more comfortable with stillness, the duration can gradually increase, and other forms of meditation can be explored. It's also essential to create a conducive environment for practice – a quiet space, free from distractions, where one can return to regularly.

Integration into Daily Life: Beyond the Cushion

While formal meditation sessions are invaluable, the ultimate goal is to integrate this heightened awareness into everyday life. Mindfulness can transform mundane activities into opportunities for practice. Whether it's while washing dishes, taking a shower, or even during a commute, each moment presents a chance to cultivate presence.

The application of meditative principles in daily life can also serve as a powerful tool for stress management. By adopting a mindful approach, one can learn to respond to situations with equanimity rather than reacting impulsively. This not only enhances personal well-being but also positively influences one's interactions with others.

In conclusion, the anatomy of meditation is vast and varied, offering a rich landscape of practices for exploration. Each form holds the potential to guide practitioners towards deeper self-awareness, peace, and compassion. By understanding the basics and engaging in regular practice, one embarks on a transformative journey that extends far beyond the meditation cushion, enriching every facet of life.

CHAPTER 7: THE ROLE OF BREATH IN MINDFULNESS

Breath, an ostensibly mundane facet of existence, wields a profound influence in the realm of mindfulness and meditation. This chapter delves into the intricate tapestry of respiration, unraveling the myriad ways in which breath serves as a cornerstone for mindfulness practices. By exploring the physiological, psychological, and philosophical dimensions of breathing, we come to appreciate its pivotal role in anchoring the present moment, regulating the emotional landscape, and fostering a deeper connection with the self.

Physiological Underpinnings of Breath in Mindfulness

Respiration is an autonomic process, primarily controlled by the brainstem, that oscillates between voluntary and involuntary control. This unique characteristic of breath makes it an exemplary anchor for mindfulness. When one directs their attention to the breath, they engage the prefrontal cortex, a region associated with higher-order brain functions. This conscious engagement allows for a modulation of the autonomic nervous system, shifting from a sympathetic ("fight or flight") to a parasympathetic ("rest and digest") dominance. The resultant effects are multifaceted, encompassing a reduction in heart rate, a lower blood pressure, and a subdued stress response. This physiological alchemy engendered by mindful breathing lays the groundwork for a serene and receptive mental state, conducive to meditation and introspection.

Psychological Significance of Breathing in Mindfulness

In the psychological realm, breath functions as a tangible representation of the transient nature of experiences. Just as the breath comes and goes, so do thoughts, emotions, and sensations. By focusing on the rhythmic ebb and flow of breath, one learns the art of detachment, observing internal phenomena without being ensnared by them. This nurtures a state of equanimity, whereby one becomes a dispassionate spectator of their inner world, fostering emotional regulation and resilience.

Moreover, the act of deep, diaphragmatic breathing triggers the release of endorphins, neurotransmitters that mitigate pain and induce a sense of well-being. This biochemical shift not only elevates one's mood but also enhances the quality of meditation, paving the way for a profound exploration of consciousness.

Philosophical and Spiritual Dimensions of Breath

The breath is imbued with rich philosophical and spiritual symbolism. In many traditions, breath is synonymous with life force or energy, known as 'prana' in Hindu philosophy and 'qi' in Chinese medicine. This life force is considered the vital energy that animates the physical form and connects the individual with the cosmos. Through mindful breathing, one taps into this universal energy, experiencing a sense of oneness and interconnectedness with all that is.

Furthermore, breath acts as a metaphorical bridge between the corporeal and the ethereal, the tangible and the transcendent. It is at once a physical act and a mystical conduit, a portal through which one can access altered states of consciousness and unearth deeper truths about the self and the universe.

Conclusion

The act of breathing, often relegated to the periphery of conscious awareness, assumes a central role in the practice of mindfulness. By honing one's focus on the breath, an individual embarks on a transformative journey, transcending the mundane to touch the sublime. The breath, in its simplicity, becomes a profound tool for self-discovery, emotional mastery, and spiritual awakening. As we navigate the labyrinth of mindfulness, breath emerges as both the compass and the path, guiding us through the intricate tapestry of our inner landscape.

CHAPTER 8: SENSORY AWARENESS AND PERCEPTION

The world reveals itself to us through an intricate dance of sensory experiences. In this chapter, we delve into the rich realm of sensory awareness and perception, elucidating their pivotal role in mindfulness and meditation practices. Our sensory apparatus acts as a bridge between the external world and our inner cognitive realms, guiding our attention and shaping our experiences. By honing our sensory perception through mindfulness, we can deepen our connection with the present moment, enhance our understanding of ourselves, and cultivate a more nuanced awareness of our surroundings.

The Quintessence of the Five Senses

Our five senses—sight, hearing, taste, smell, and touch—are the primary means through which we engage with the world. Each sense is a gateway, offering unique insights and nuances about our environment. Mindfulness practices often begin with a focus on these sensory portals, inviting practitioners to observe the world in its raw form, devoid of judgment or interpretation.

Sight provides us with shapes, colors, and movements, painting a vivid tapestry of the world before us. Hearing captures vibrations and translates them into sounds, from the gentle rustle of leaves to the cacophony of urban life. Taste and smell work in concert, offering a symphony of flavors and scents that can evoke memories and emotions. Touch connects us physically to the world, conveying texture, temperature, and pressure.

Attuning to Sensory Subtleties

In mindfulness, the emphasis is not just on the senses themselves, but on our awareness of them. It's about noticing the subtleties—the faintest hint of jasmine in the air, the slight roughness of fabric against skin, the distant melody of a songbird. By attuning our attention to these subtle sensory details, we cultivate a heightened state of awareness. This practice serves to anchor us in the present moment, pulling our minds away from the relentless chatter and into the tranquility of now.

Sensory Mindfulness Exercises

To facilitate the deepening of sensory awareness, various mindfulness exercises can be practiced. These exercises are designed to refine our perception and bring our focus to the immediacy of our sensory experiences.

1. **Mindful Observation**: Choose an object and observe it with all your senses. Notice its color, texture, and any sounds it might make. If applicable, observe its scent and taste. Engage with it as if for the first time.
2. **Sound Bath Meditation**: Close your eyes and allow yourself to become immersed in the sounds around you. Observe the layers of sounds without labeling or judging them. Let them wash over you like waves, noticing the rise and fall of each sound.

3. **Sensory Walk**: Take a walk and dedicate your attention to your senses. Feel the air against your skin, notice the scents that drift by, observe the colors and movements around you, and tune in to the symphony of sounds.

By integrating sensory awareness into our mindfulness practice, we not only enrich our meditation experience but also enhance our perceptual acuity. This heightened sensitivity can transform ordinary moments into a tapestry of wonder, imbuing our daily lives with a deeper sense of presence and connection.

This chapter invites readers to explore the world through their senses, encouraging a playful curiosity and attentiveness. By cultivating sensory mindfulness, we open ourselves to a richer, more vibrant experience of life, where every moment is an opportunity for discovery and connection.

CHAPTER 9: MINDFULNESS AND EMOTIONS

In this exploration of the mindful spectrum, we delve into the profound interconnectedness between mindfulness and our emotional tapestry. The human emotional experience, a complex whirlwind of feelings and reactions, is deeply intertwined with our cognitive processes. As we embark on this chapter, we shall unfurl the layers of this connection and understand how the practice of mindfulness serves not just as a coping mechanism but also as a transformative tool in regulating and understanding our emotions.

The Emotional Landscape

Our emotional spectrum is vast, encompassing a myriad of feelings ranging from the depths of despair to the peaks of ecstasy. These emotions are not merely responses to external stimuli, but are also deeply rooted in our internal cognitive landscape. They influence our thoughts, actions, and overall well-being. Recognizing this influence is crucial in understanding the role of mindfulness in emotional regulation.

Mindfulness: A Beacon in Emotional Turbulence

Mindfulness, in its essence, is the practice of being present and fully engaged with whatever we're doing, free from distraction or judgment, and aware of our thoughts and feelings without getting caught up in them. This practice becomes particularly pivotal in the context of emotional regulation.

1. **Observation without Judgment**: At the heart of mindfulness is the ability to observe our emotions without getting entangled in them. This objective observation allows us to recognize our feelings without labeling them as 'good' or 'bad'. This non-judgmental stance is the first step toward emotional regulation.

2. **Response vs. Reaction**: Mindfulness teaches us the difference between responding and reacting. While reactions are often immediate and laden with unexamined emotions, responses are thoughtful and considerate. Mindfulness enables us to take a pause before responding, allowing us to deal with emotional situations with clarity and wisdom.

3. **Understanding Emotional Impermanence**: Emotions, by nature, are transient. Mindfulness practices instill the understanding that just like a storm, emotions too shall pass. This understanding fosters resilience and reduces the propensity to be overwhelmed by intense emotions.

Emotions as Pathways to Self-Discovery

Mindfulness not only helps in managing emotions but also acts as a gateway to deeper self-discovery and personal growth. By observing our emotional responses, we can gain insights into our patterns, triggers, and habits. This introspective journey illuminates our inner world, fostering emotional intelligence and self-awareness.

1. **Patterns and Triggers**: Through consistent mindfulness practice, we begin to notice recurring

patterns in our emotional responses. Identifying these patterns helps in understanding the underlying triggers, paving the way for transformative growth.

2. **Cultivating Emotional Intelligence**: Emotional intelligence is the ability to recognize, understand, and manage our own emotions while also being empathetic to the emotions of others. Mindfulness cultivates emotional intelligence by enhancing our awareness and control over our emotional responses.

3. **Enhancing Empathy and Compassion**: Mindfulness opens the door to deeper empathy and compassion, both for ourselves and for others. By understanding our own emotions, we become more attuned to the emotional states of those around us, fostering healthier and more meaningful relationships.

Integrating Mindfulness into Emotional Well-being

Incorporating mindfulness into our daily routine can have profound effects on our emotional well-being. Simple practices like mindful breathing, meditation, and present-moment awareness can be woven into the fabric of our daily lives, offering a sanctuary of calm in the tumultuous sea of emotions.

1. **Mindful Breathing**: This simple yet powerful practice involves focusing on the breath, observing its rhythm, and using it as an anchor to the present moment. This technique can be especially useful during moments of emotional distress.

2. **Daily Meditation**: Setting aside time for daily meditation can significantly improve emotional regulation. It provides a structured approach to mindfulness, fostering a deeper connection with our emotional self.

3. **Present-Moment Awareness**: Engaging fully with the present moment, whether it's while eating, walking, or listening, can help in recognizing and savoring the positive emotions, while also calmly acknowledging the negative ones.

This chapter has journeyed through the rich tapestry of emotions and the transformative role of mindfulness in emotional regulation and self-discovery. Embracing mindfulness is akin to embarking on a voyage across the emotional seas, with awareness as our compass and acceptance as our anchor. As we continue to weave through the concepts of mindfulness, let us carry forward the understanding of emotions as not just responses but as profound teachers and guides on our path to self-awareness and growth.

CHAPTER 10: THE BODY-SCAN METHOD

Embarking on the journey of mindfulness brings us to an intricate technique known as the Body-Scan Method. This chapter delves into the nuances of this practice, unraveling its benefits and guiding readers through the steps to effectively incorporate it into their mindfulness regimen.

The Essence of the Body-Scan Method

At its core, the Body-Scan Method is a mindfulness practice that involves paying detailed attention to different parts of the body, acknowledging any sensations or feelings that arise, without attempting to change or judge them. It is a form of meditation that fosters a deep connection between the mind and the body, allowing practitioners to develop a heightened awareness of their physical selves. This method serves as a foundational practice in many mindfulness-based interventions, such as Mindfulness-Based Stress Reduction (MBSR), due to its profound impact on both mental and physical well-being.

Unveiling the Process

The practice of the Body-Scan Method generally follows a structured progression, although it allows for personal adaptations. It typically involves the following steps:

1. **Finding a Comfortable Position**: Begin by lying down on your back in a comfortable position. You can choose to lie on a yoga mat, a bed, or any flat surface that provides support. Ensure that your body is in a neutral position, with your arms resting by your sides, palms facing upward, and your legs slightly apart.

2. **Initiating the Practice**: Close your eyes and take a few deep breaths. Allow the rhythm of your breathing to anchor your focus, drawing your attention inward.

3. **Directing Awareness to the Body**: Gradually shift your attention to your body, starting from the tips of your toes. Acknowledge any sensations, such as warmth, coolness, tingling, or even the absence of sensations. Maintain a non-judgmental attitude towards whatever you perceive.

4. **Scanning the Body**: Slowly guide your awareness up through your body, part by part—feet, ankles, calves, knees, thighs, hips, abdomen, chest, back, arms, hands, neck, and head. Spend some time on each area, observing with curiosity.

5. **Breathing into Each Part**: As you focus on each body part, visualize breathing into that area. Imagine the breath bringing relaxation and release with each exhale.

6. **Concluding the Practice**: After completing the scan, allow your awareness to encompass your entire body as a whole. Take a few more deep breaths, then gradually bring movement back into your body by wiggling your fingers and toes. When you feel ready, slowly open your eyes and acclimate back to your surroundings.

Transformative Effects

Engaging in the Body-Scan Method offers a multitude of transformative effects that extend beyond mere relaxation. These include:

- **Enhanced Body Awareness**: Regular practice of the Body-Scan Method cultivates a more profound and nuanced awareness of bodily sensations, contributing to an improved mind-body connection.
- **Stress Reduction**: By focusing on the present moment and observing bodily sensations without judgment, practitioners can experience a significant reduction in stress and anxiety levels.
- **Emotional Regulation**: The practice encourages individuals to acknowledge and accept their emotional states, leading to improved emotional regulation and resilience.
- **Pain Management**: Research has shown that the Body-Scan Method can be particularly effective in managing chronic pain, as it shifts the perception of pain and helps in developing coping strategies.

Incorporating the Practice into Daily Life

Integrating the Body-Scan Method into your daily routine need not be a daunting task. Even a short, 10-minute session can yield benefits. For those new to the practice, guided audio recordings are a valuable resource, providing step-by-step instructions and pacing. Over time, as familiarity with the process grows, practitioners may find themselves able to conduct body scans independently, even in shorter durations or in different postures, such as sitting or standing.

In conclusion, the Body-Scan Method is a versatile and powerful tool within the mindfulness arsenal. Its simplicity belies its profound ability to foster a harmonious relationship between mind and body, serving as a gateway to deeper self-awareness and well-being. As we progress further into the realms of mindfulness and meditation, let the principles and practices of the Body-Scan Method be a beacon, guiding us towards a more attentive, compassionate, and grounded existence.

CHAPTER 11: SIMPLE MEDITATION RITUALS

Meditation, often perceived as a solemn, solitary activity, is rich with diverse rituals that enhance the experience and imbue it with a sense of sacredness and structure. These rituals, far from being mere formalities, serve as vital instruments in harmonizing the mind, body, and spirit, paving a serene pathway to the deeper realms of mindfulness. In this chapter, we explore simple yet profound meditation rituals that beginners can seamlessly integrate into their practice, transforming their journey into an experience brimming with intention, focus, and reverence.

The Sanctity of Space

The quintessence of a meditation ritual begins with the sanctification of space. This process is not merely a physical arrangement but an act of consecrating the area, making it conducive to mindfulness and introspection. It involves choosing a spot that resonates with tranquility and minimal distractions. The space need not be expansive or extravagantly adorned; a simple, uncluttered corner suffices, as long as it offers a semblance of solitude and calm. Adorning this space with elements that evoke serenity—be it a soft mat, cushions, or subtle incense—can enhance the ambiance, making it inviting and comfortable for prolonged periods of meditation.

The Prelude of Purification

Purification rituals serve as a symbolic cleansing of the mind and body, preparing the practitioner for an undistracted entry into a meditative state. This could be as straightforward as washing hands and face with cool water, signifying the washing away of external concerns and grounding oneself in the present. Some might find lighting a candle or incense beneficial, as the act of igniting a flame can symbolize the kindling of inner awareness. The gentle aroma that pervades the air can act as an anchor, gently guiding the mind back when it wanders.

The Cadence of Breathing

Before delving into the depths of meditation, initiating a breathing ritual sets the rhythm for the practice. Conscious breathing acts as a bridge, connecting the corporeal to the cognitive, the tangible to the intangible. Beginning with a few deep breaths, feeling the air fill the lungs and then slowly releasing it, helps in centering the mind. This simple act of attentiveness to breath can significantly reduce the clamor of thoughts, ushering in a state of physiological and psychological relaxation conducive to meditation.

The Harmony of Chants

Chanting, an optional yet potent ritual, can be incorporated to enrich the meditative experience. The vibrational quality of chants, often manifested as mantras, transcends mere auditory stimulation, resonating within the practitioner on a profound level. The repetitive nature of chanting fosters a sense of focus and presence, creating a rhythmic cadence that can lead to deeper states of meditation. Even simple words or phrases, chosen for their personal significance, can serve as powerful mantras, imbuing the practice with intention and depth.

The Anchor of Visualization

For those who find the abstract nature of meditation challenging, incorporating a visualization ritual can serve as a tangible anchor. Picturing a serene landscape, a radiant light, or any imagery that evokes peace can serve as a focal point, providing the mind with a refuge from distracting thoughts. Visualization serves as a gentle guide, leading the practitioner through the terrains of their inner world, often revealing insights and fostering a profound sense of connectedness with the self.

Concluding with Gratitude

Concluding the meditation with a ritual of gratitude gracefully seals the practice. Acknowledging the time set aside for self-care, the insights gained, and even the mere act of being present, instills a sense of appreciation and fulfillment. It reinforces the understanding that every moment spent in meditation is a step towards greater self-awareness and equanimity.

In essence, these simple meditation rituals serve as sacred threads, weaving together a tapestry of intention, presence, and reverence. They are not rigid structures but fluid practices that can be tailored to resonate with the individual practitioner. Integrating these rituals into one's meditation practice can transform it from a routine activity into a holistic and enriching journey, paving the way for a deeper connection with the self and the profound wisdom it holds.

CHAPTER 12: OBSERVING THOUGHT PATTERNS

Embarking on a journey of mindfulness involves not only a deep connection with the breath and the body but also a keen understanding of the landscape of our thoughts. In this chapter, we shall navigate the intricate pathways of our minds, learning how to observe our thought patterns through the lens of mindfulness. This process serves as a pivotal step in enhancing our cognitive well-being and achieving a state of mental clarity.

The Nature of Thoughts

Thoughts are the constant chatter of the mind, an endless stream that shapes our perceptions, influences our emotions, and dictates our actions. They are spontaneous, often arising without our conscious control, and can range from fleeting notions to profound ruminations. However, the essence of mindfulness lies in the realization that thoughts are transient and do not define our true selves. By observing them objectively, we can gain insights into our habitual mental patterns and develop a more balanced perspective.

Mindfulness and the Observation of Thoughts

The practice of observing thought patterns is rooted in the foundational principles of mindfulness. It involves detaching ourselves from our thoughts, perceiving them as mere events in the mind rather than intrinsic truths. This detachment does not imply disinterest or suppression; rather, it embodies an attitude of non-judgmental awareness. By cultivating such an observational stance, we enable ourselves to witness the ebb and flow of thoughts without becoming ensnared by them.

Techniques for Observing Thought Patterns

Observing our thoughts is a skill that can be honed through various mindfulness techniques. Here are some methods that facilitate this process:

1. Mindful Breathing: Anchor your awareness in the rhythm of your breath. When thoughts arise, simply acknowledge them and gently bring your focus back to the breath. This practice helps in disengaging from the pull of thoughts and cultivating centeredness.

2. Labeling Thoughts: As thoughts surface, mentally assign a label to them, such as "planning," "remembering," or "judging." This technique helps in recognizing the nature of thoughts and prevents entanglement with their content.

3. Visualization: Imagine your thoughts as leaves floating down a stream or clouds drifting across the sky. Visualize yourself as an observer on the bank or under the vast expanse, watching them pass by without attachment.

4. Open Awareness Meditation: Sit quietly and allow thoughts to arise naturally. Observe them with an open and accepting attitude, letting them come and go without resistance.

Benefits of Observing Thought Patterns

The practice of observing thought patterns offers numerous benefits:

- It fosters self-awareness, enabling us to recognize unhelpful thought patterns and tendencies toward rumination or negative self-talk.
- It enhances emotional regulation by preventing us from becoming overwhelmed by our thoughts, especially during times of stress or anxiety.
- It contributes to mental clarity, as we learn to distinguish between useful thoughts that require attention and irrelevant ones that can be let go.
- It cultivates a sense of inner peace and equanimity, as we become less reactive to the fluctuations of the mind.

In conclusion, observing our thought patterns through mindfulness is a transformative exercise that empowers us to navigate the terrain of our minds with greater wisdom and compassion. It is a journey of introspection that leads to a deeper understanding of ourselves and our cognitive processes, fostering a harmonious relationship between our inner and outer worlds. As we progress on this path, we come to realize that we are not our thoughts; rather, we are the conscious presence that observes them, serene and unswayed amidst the ceaseless chatter of the mind.

CHAPTER 13: MINDFUL EATING AND CONSUMPTION

Embarking on a journey through the nuanced landscape of mindful eating, this chapter delves into the intimate relationship between mindfulness and consumption, exploring how the conscious choices we make about our food can profoundly influence not only our physical well-being but also our mental clarity and emotional balance.

The Philosophy of Mindful Eating

Mindful eating is an ancient practice, deeply rooted in the philosophy of being present with one's food. It involves paying full attention to the experience of eating and drinking, both inside and outside the body. Mindful eating brings awareness to the colors, smells, textures, flavors, temperatures, and even the sounds of our food. It is an acknowledgment of the interdependent network that culminates in a meal: from the sun, soil, and water that nurture the ingredients to the human efforts that bring them to the table. By eating mindfully, we turn an ordinary routine into a moment of reflection, gratitude, and a celebration of sensory experience.

The Practice: Techniques and Benefits

At its core, mindful eating is about using mindfulness to reach a state of full attention to one's experiences, cravings, and physical cues when eating. Here are some fundamental techniques to practice mindful eating:

1. **Eating Slowly and Without Distraction**: Engage fully with the act of eating, without the interference of television, computers, or books. Allow yourself to experience your food with all your senses.

2. **Listening to Physical Hunger Cues**: Learn to listen to your body and eat only until you are full.

3. **Distinguishing between True Hunger and Non-Hunger Triggers for Eating**: Develop an understanding of the emotional, environmental, and social cues that trigger eating even when you're not hungry.

4. **Engaging Your Senses**: Notice the colors, textures, scents, and flavors of your food.

5. **Learning to Cope with Guilt and Anxiety about Food**: Accept that there is no right or wrong way to eat but varying degrees of awareness surrounding the experience of food.

6. **Appreciating Your Food**: Pause before you begin eating to express gratitude for the meal before you.

The benefits of mindful eating are multifaceted. It can lead to a healthier relationship with food, characterized by a reduction in overeating, an increase in enjoyment of food, and a greater sense of control over eating habits. Mindful eating can also lead to better digestion, as it encourages slower eating, which allows for better chewing and easier digestion.

Mindful Consumption Beyond Food

Extending beyond the realm of eating, mindful consumption also pertains to the broader choices we make as consumers. It encompasses an awareness of the environmental, health, and life consequences of our purchases. Mindful consumption invites us to consider the lifecycle of the products we buy—from their creation to their disposal—and to make choices that are in harmony with our values and the well-being of the planet. It's an invitation to ask ourselves whether what we're consuming is nourishing us and the world around us or whether it's contributing to harm.

In a world where the pace of life is ever-increasing and our attention is pulled in multiple directions, mindful eating and consumption serve as grounding practices. They remind us to slow down, to savor the moment, and to make conscious choices that align with our deepest values. As we integrate these practices into our daily lives, we cultivate a deeper connection to ourselves, our community, and the planet that sustains us.

CHAPTER 14: YOGA AND PHYSICAL MINDFULNESS

As we traverse the enlightening path of "Noetic Scrying: Divining Through Cognitive States", we approach a chapter dedicated to the ancient practice of yoga and its intrinsic connection with physical mindfulness. This chapter will explore how the deliberate movements and poses of yoga can cultivate a heightened state of awareness, aligning the body and mind in a harmonious dance of presence.

Yoga: A Brief Historical Tapestry

The roots of yoga stretch back thousands of years, intertwining with the spiritual soil of ancient India. Initially, yoga served as a meditative practice, a tool for spiritual growth, and a method for understanding the universe and the individual's place within it. Over time, the practice evolved, incorporating physical postures, known as asanas, and breath control, pranayama, to enhance the meditative experience.

Yoga's migration to the Western world brought a renewed focus on its physical aspects, often overshadowing its deep spiritual and mental roots. However, at its core, yoga remains a practice that unites the body, mind, and spirit, providing a platform for physical mindfulness.

Asanas: The Physical Language of Yoga

Asanas, the physical postures of yoga, serve as a conduit for mindfulness. Each pose is a deliberate act, an invitation to focus intently on the alignment of limbs, the distribution of weight, and the rhythm of breath. This heightened physical awareness brings a unique clarity of mind, as extraneous thoughts are pared away, leaving only the present moment and the sensations it holds.

Yoga poses range from the simple to the complex, each with its own set of benefits and challenges. For beginners, poses such as Tadasana (Mountain Pose) or Balasana (Child's Pose) offer a gentle entry into the world of yoga, emphasizing stability and grounding. More advanced practitioners may engage with asanas like Sirsasana (Headstand) or Adho Mukha Vrksasana (Handstand), which challenge balance and invert the usual perspectives, both physically and mentally.

Pranayama: The Breath of Life

Pranayama, or the control of breath, is a fundamental aspect of yoga that directly influences one's state of mindfulness. Breath is the bridge between the body and mind, a rhythmic tide that ebbs and flows with our emotions and thoughts. By consciously regulating the breath, one can calm the restless mind and attune to the present moment.

Practices such as Anulom Vilom (Alternate Nostril Breathing) or Kapalabhati (Skull Shining Breath) have profound effects on the nervous system, reducing stress and promoting mental clarity. These breathing techniques are not mere exercises; they are rituals of mindfulness, each inhalation a step deeper into awareness, each exhalation a release of the trivial and transient.

Yoga and Mindfulness: A Symbiotic Symphony

The synergy of yoga and mindfulness is a dance of intent and attention. As one flows through the asanas, the mind is encouraged to remain vigilant, aware of the subtleties of movement and the whispers of the body. This union of physical practice and mental focus is the essence of mindfulness in yoga.

The practice of yoga transcends mere physical exercise; it is a holistic journey that encompasses the body, mind, and spirit. It invites practitioners to explore the depths of their being, to confront their limitations, and to embrace the present moment with an open heart and a tranquil mind.

In conclusion, yoga is not just a series of postures; it is a philosophy, a way of life that advocates for a mindful existence. By engaging in the physical practice of yoga, one embarks on a path of self-discovery, learning to navigate the intricate landscapes of the mind and body with grace and awareness. Through the lens of yoga, physical mindfulness becomes a profound tool for personal growth and a stepping stone toward the ultimate goal of noetic scrying: divining the depths of one's cognitive states to unearth the hidden treasures of the self.

CHAPTER 15: ZEN AND THE ART OF PRESENCE

Zen Buddhism, a tradition steeped in the essence of simplicity, directness, and presence, offers a profound path to mindfulness and meditation. As a practice that emphasizes sitting meditation, known as 'zazen', Zen hones the art of presence, nurturing an awareness that is both penetrating and expansive. This chapter delves into the philosophical underpinnings of Zen, its meditation techniques, and how it fosters a state of mindfulness that can transform one's perception of reality.

Philosophical Underpinnings of Zen

Zen Buddhism, which emerged from the confluence of Indian Buddhism and Chinese Taoism, carries a unique philosophical framework that underscores the importance of direct experience over intellectual abstraction. Its teachings are often encapsulated in brief, paradoxical statements or koans, designed not to educate the mind, but to short-circuit it, propelling the practitioner into a state of direct awareness.

The fundamental Zen philosophy orbits around the notion of 'sunyata' or emptiness, suggesting that phenomena are devoid of an intrinsic, immutable nature. This view encourages the practitioner to release attachments to fixed ideas and to perceive the impermanent and interdependent nature of reality. In doing so, Zen fosters a deep presence and attentiveness to the unfolding moment, a cornerstone of mindfulness.

Zen Meditation Techniques

At the heart of Zen practice is 'zazen', a form of seated meditation that is both the means and the expression of enlightenment. Unlike some forms of meditation that involve concentration on a particular object or mantra, zazen emphasizes 'shikantaza', which can be translated as 'just sitting'. This technique is not goal-oriented; it is the cultivation of a state of alert, non-discriminative awareness. Practitioners sit with a straight posture, eyes half-closed, and focus on the natural rhythm of their breath while letting thoughts and sensations arise and fade without attachment.

Another key aspect of Zen meditation is walking meditation, or 'kinhin', which complements the stillness of zazen. Kinhin involves slow, deliberate walking, with mindfulness directed towards the physical sensations of each step. This practice cultivates presence in motion, integrating the mindfulness cultivated during zazen into movement and, by extension, into the dynamism of daily life.

Zen and Mindfulness in Daily Life

The Zen approach to mindfulness extends far beyond the cushion; it permeates every aspect of daily life. The practice of 'samu', or work practice, is an integral part of Zen monastic life, where mundane activities such as cooking, cleaning, or gardening are performed with the same mindfulness and presence as zazen. This embodiment of mindfulness in everyday actions illuminates the Zen teaching that there is no separation between the sacred and the mundane, between meditation and ordinary life.

Incorporating Zen principles into daily life can transform mundane activities into opportunities for mindfulness practice. By bringing full attention to the task at hand, whether it's washing dishes or listening to a friend, one can cultivate a sense of presence that permeates every moment. This practice helps dissolve the barriers between 'meditation' and 'life', revealing the profound truth that each moment, no matter how ordinary, is a doorway to the sacred.

In conclusion, Zen Buddhism offers a rich and profound path to mindfulness and meditation, characterized by its emphasis on presence, direct experience, and the integration of mindfulness into every facet of life. Its practices and teachings provide invaluable insights into the nature of mind and reality, guiding practitioners toward a deeper understanding and appreciation of the present moment. As we transition to the intermediate chapters of this book, the principles and practices of Zen will continue to serve as a foundation, a touchstone for the exploration of more complex and nuanced dimensions of mindfulness and meditation.

CHAPTER 16: METACOGNITION: THINKING ABOUT THINKING

Metacognition, a term derived from the Greek root "meta" meaning "beyond," and "cognition" referring to "thinking," delves into the realm of thinking about one's own thinking processes. In the context of mindfulness and noetic scrying, metacognition becomes a pivotal bridge, connecting self-awareness with heightened cognitive states.

The Layers of Metacognition

Metacognition encompasses two primary layers: knowledge about cognition and regulation of cognition. The former relates to one's understanding of how cognitive processes operate, including awareness of one's cognitive strengths and limitations. The latter, regulation of cognition, involves the orchestration of cognitive strategies, monitoring one's performance, and making adjustments as needed. In the practice of mindfulness, these layers are deeply intertwined with the act of introspection and self-reflection, forming a feedback loop that enhances mental clarity and focus.

Metacognitive Strategies in Mindfulness

One might wonder how metacognition translates into practical application within the realms of mindfulness and meditation. Here are several strategies:

1. **Self-monitoring:** A cornerstone of mindfulness, self-monitoring involves observing one's thoughts, emotions, and sensations without judgment. Through metacognitive awareness, practitioners become attuned to their cognitive patterns, identifying habits, biases, and triggers.
2. **Goal Setting:** In mindfulness practice, setting clear intentions serves as a guidepost. Metacognitively aware individuals can craft goals that are aligned with their cognitive tendencies, optimizing their practice for personal growth and insight.
3. **Strategy Evaluation:** A metacognitive practitioner might employ different mindfulness techniques, continuously assessing their effectiveness. This could involve alternating between focused attention and open monitoring meditation, gauging which brings greater tranquility or clarity in different contexts.

Metacognition's Role in Enhancing Mindfulness

Metacognition holds a mirror to our mental operations, allowing us to become architects of our own minds. Through cultivating metacognitive skills, mindfulness practitioners can deepen their practice, transitioning from passive observers of their mental landscape to active participants in shaping it. This heightened awareness of one's cognitive machinery can lead to more effective mindfulness practices, as individuals can tailor their approach to align with their unique cognitive profiles.

Metacognition and Noetic Scrying

In the pursuit of noetic scrying—divination through cognitive states—metacognition serves as a powerful ally. It enables practitioners to navigate their inner world with a cartographer's precision, charting a course through the layers of consciousness. By understanding the mechanics of their thinking, individuals engaged in noetic scrying can more adeptly interpret the symbols and insights that arise from the depths of their mind, transforming abstract cognition into tangible wisdom.

In conclusion, metacognition is not merely an abstract concept, but a dynamic and integral component of mindfulness and meditation. By embracing the introspective journey of thinking about thinking, one unlocks a higher echelon of cognitive clarity and self-mastery. As we transition from the introductory chapters into more complex territories, the principles of metacognition will continue to serve as a guiding light, illuminating the path toward deeper understanding and enlightenment.

CHAPTER 17: MINDFULNESS AND NEURAL PLASTICITY

As we delve into the intermediate chapters of "Noetic Scrying: Divining Through Cognitive States," we enter a realm where the bridges between the physical and the metaphysical begin to intertwine more evidently. Chapter 17 explores the fascinating concept of neural plasticity and its profound relationship with mindfulness practices. This intricate liaison between the mind's malleability and the practice of mindfulness underscores an extraordinary potential: the power to reshape our very brain structure through intentional cognitive practices.

The Alchemy of the Mind

Neural plasticity, or neuroplasticity, is the brain's ability to reorganize itself by forming new neural connections throughout life. This capability is not just a feature of the young or the learning; it's an enduring aspect of the human brain. Mindfulness, with its roots firmly planted in the fertile soil of introspection and self-awareness, acts as a gardener of the mind, pruning and nurturing these connections.

When we engage in mindfulness practices, we're not just stilling the mind or seeking tranquility; we're partaking in a sophisticated form of cerebral architecture. Each moment of mindful awareness, each breath taken with intention, strengthens and creates new pathways in our brains. These pathways can lead to enhanced cognitive abilities, emotional regulation, and even a deeper understanding of the self and the universe.

Mindfulness as a Sculptor

To understand the scope of neuroplasticity's influence under the guidance of mindfulness, one must consider how consistent practice can sculpt the brain. Research has shown that mindfulness can lead to an increase in gray matter in areas of the brain associated with memory, learning, and emotion regulation. This isn't just an abstract improvement; it translates to tangible benefits in daily life, such as better decision-making, improved concentration, and a heightened capacity for empathy.

Moreover, mindfulness practices have been associated with a decrease in the gray matter in the amygdala, a region of the brain involved in the processing of emotions like fear and stress. This neural downscaling can lead to a more balanced emotional life, providing a buffer against the storms of anxiety and overreaction.

The Resilient Brain

An essential aspect of mindfulness's impact on neural plasticity is the cultivation of resilience. Mindfulness doesn't just build a brain that's better at certain tasks or more balanced emotionally; it forges a brain that's better equipped to handle the inevitable adversities of life.

Through mindfulness, we can train our brains to respond to stress in healthier ways. We can diminish the neurological pathways that lead to panic and despair, and strengthen those that lead to calmness and rationality. This isn't just about feeling better in the moment; it's about creating a durable foundation for long-term mental health.

Summary

CHAPTER 17 INVITES READERS ON A JOURNEY THROUGH THE MALLEABLE CORRIDORS OF THEIR OWN MINDS, ILLUMINATING THE PROFOUND IMPACT THAT MINDFULNESS CAN HAVE ON NEURAL PLASTICITY. THIS EXPLORATION REVEALS THAT

THROUGH MINDFULNESS, WE'RE NOT JUST OBSERVERS OF OUR COGNITIVE LANDSCAPES; WE'RE ACTIVE SCULPTORS, CAPABLE OF RESHAPING THE VERY SUBSTANCE OF OUR BRAINS. AS WE CLOSE THIS CHAPTER, WE STAND AT THE THRESHOLD OF AN EMPOWERING

REALIZATION: OUR MENTAL AND EMOTIONAL DESTINIES MAY BE MORE IN OUR OWN HANDS THAN WE EVER IMAGINED.

CHAPTER 18: TRANSCENDENTAL MEDITATION EXPLORED

Transcendental Meditation (TM), a practice that has gained a significant following since its inception in the mid-20th century, stands as a cornerstone in the pantheon of meditative disciplines. Unlike other forms of meditation that advocate concentration or contemplation, Transcendental Meditation hinges on the effortless transcendence beyond thought, delving into a profound state of restful awareness. This chapter delves into the intricate tapestry of TM, unraveling its techniques, its physiological and psychological impacts, and its distinct place in the broader landscape of mindfulness practices.

The Technique and Its Unfolding

Transcendental Meditation is practiced for twenty minutes twice a day while sitting comfortably with closed eyes. The method involves the use of a personalized mantra, a specific sound or phrase given to the practitioner by a certified TM teacher. This mantra, devoid of meaning to preclude any distraction, serves as a vehicle for the mind to naturally and effortlessly descend into quieter levels of thought, eventually transcending thought altogether to reach a state of pure consciousness.

This technique is rooted in the belief that the deepest level of consciousness is a field of infinite creativity and intelligence. By tapping into this reservoir, practitioners of TM claim to enliven these qualities within themselves, leading to a myriad of benefits that span from deep relaxation to enhanced cognitive functions.

Physiological Ripples of TM

The physiological impacts of Transcendental Meditation are measurable and multifaceted. Research indicates that during TM practice, the body enters a state of profound rest, more restorative than sleep. This is characterized by a significant drop in metabolic rate, reduced stress hormone levels, and a distinct pattern of brain wave coherence. These changes are associated with a host of health benefits, including lowered blood pressure, reduced risk of heart disease, and amelioration of anxiety and depression.

Moreover, the state of restful alertness achieved during TM has been linked to enhanced neural plasticity. This is the brain's ability to reorganize itself, forming new neural connections throughout life. Such a capacity is instrumental in learning, memory, and the self-regulation of cognitive and emotional processes.

Psychological Expanses and Potential Pitfalls

On the psychological front, regular practitioners of TM report increased self-awareness, emotional stability, and a general sense of well-being. Some studies suggest that TM may have a positive effect on psychological disorders, including attention deficit hyperactivity disorder (ADHD) and post-traumatic stress disorder (PTSD). However, it is essential to approach these findings with a degree of caution, as research on TM, like many areas in the psychological sciences, is not without its methodological criticisms.

Furthermore, it is crucial to consider the individual variability in response to any meditative practice. While many find TM to be a profoundly transformative technique, others may not resonate with its approach. It is the responsibility of each practitioner to attune to their own experiences and needs, seeking guidance and adjusting their practices accordingly.

Transcendental Meditation within the Meditation Mosaic

Transcendental Meditation occupies a unique space within the meditation mosaic. Its effortless approach contrasts with practices that emphasize focused attention or contemplative inquiry. This distinction is not indicative of superiority or inferiority but rather underscores the rich diversity within meditative disciplines. The suitability of TM, as with any practice, is ultimately determined by the practitioner's intentions, comfort, and experiences.

In conclusion, Transcendental Meditation presents a pathway to transcendence through effortless meditation. By exploring its techniques, physiological impacts, and psychological benefits, practitioners can discern its role in their personal journey toward mindfulness and self-discovery. As we continue to navigate the intricate web of meditative practices, it becomes increasingly clear that each strand, each technique, contributes to a larger, more harmonious picture of human potential and consciousness.

CHAPTER 19: BIOFEEDBACK AND MINDFULNESS

Biofeedback: A Technological Extension of Mindfulness

In the convergence of modern technology and ancient mindfulness practices, biofeedback emerges as a fascinating synthesis, bringing a quantifiable dimension to the esoteric realm of inner awareness. This chapter delves into the intricate relationship between biofeedback and mindfulness, elucidating how biofeedback serves as both a tool and a testament to the profound impact of mindfulness practices on the human psyche and physiology.

Understanding Biofeedback

At its core, biofeedback is a process that involves monitoring physiological functions such as heart rate, muscle tension, and brainwave patterns, typically through sensors attached to the body. This data is fed back to the individual in real-time, usually via a computer screen or auditory signals. The principle behind biofeedback is that, by being aware of these physiological states, individuals can learn to exert control over them, leading to enhanced well-being and health.

In the context of mindfulness, biofeedback can be seen

as an external manifestation of internal processes. Where mindfulness encourages an inward attunement to bodily sensations and mental states, biofeedback externalizes this awareness, presenting it in a form that can be objectively observed, measured, and, ultimately, harnessed.

Biofeedback and Mindfulness: A Symbiotic Relationship

Biofeedback and mindfulness share a symbiotic relationship, each enriching the other. Mindfulness practitioners can utilize biofeedback to gain deeper insights into their physiological responses during meditation, enhancing their ability to fine-tune their practice. Conversely, biofeedback can benefit from the heightened body-mind awareness cultivated through mindfulness, leading to more effective self-regulation.

One of the most compelling aspects of biofeedback is its ability to make the invisible, visible. For instance, the subtle shifts in brainwave patterns during meditation, often imperceptible to the meditator, can be brought to light through EEG biofeedback. This revelation can be profoundly validating, reinforcing the tangible benefits of mindfulness practices.

Applications and Implications

The applications of biofeedback in the realm of mindfulness are diverse. It has been employed to aid in stress reduction, alleviate anxiety, and even enhance cognitive performance. One notable example is the use of Heart Rate Variability (HRV) biofeedback, which measures the time interval between heartbeats. By consciously altering their breath patterns during mindfulness practices, individuals can influence their HRV, which is linked to improved emotional regulation and resilience.

Beyond individual applications, biofeedback has implications for the broader understanding of mindfulness. It provides empirical evidence of the physiological changes that occur during meditation, offering a bridge between subjective experiences and objective data. This validation is invaluable in the context of mindfulness as a therapeutic intervention, bolstering its credibility in the scientific and medical communities.

In essence, biofeedback extends the scope of mindfulness from an introspective practice to an interactive dialogue between the internal and external realms. It underscores the profound interplay between mind, body, and technology, offering a glimpse into the potential of this synergy for fostering deeper self-awareness and well-being.

As we navigate the complex interplay of biofeedback and mindfulness, we are reminded of the ever-evolving landscape of human consciousness. The fusion of ancient wisdom and modern technology not only enriches our understanding of mindfulness but also expands the horizons of what is possible in the realm of personal growth and healing.

CHAPTER 20: MINDFULNESS-BASED STRESS REDUCTION (MBSR)

Embarking on a journey through the labyrinthine corridors of mindfulness leads us to a juncture where science coalesces with ancient wisdom, forming a therapeutic amalgam known as Mindfulness-Based Stress Reduction (MBSR). This chapter navigates the theoretical underpinnings, practical applications, and transformative potential of MBSR, providing a comprehensive understanding of how this modality harnesses the essence of mindfulness to combat stress, enhance well-being, and foster psychological resilience.

The Genesis and Evolution of MBSR

Mindfulness-Based Stress Reduction was birthed in the late 1970s, emerging from the vision and clinical expertise of Dr. Jon Kabat-Zinn. It was conceived at the University of Massachusetts Medical Center with the aim of aiding patients grappling with chronic pain and stress. The foundational premise of MBSR is rooted in the cultivation of mindfulness, a state of active, open attention to the present moment, free from judgment and reactivity. This pioneering program has burgeoned into a widely recognized and empirically validated intervention, transcending clinical settings and permeating diverse sectors of society.

The Core Framework of MBSR

At its core, MBSR is structured as an eight-week program, meticulously designed to facilitate a gradual yet profound transformation in participants' relationship with stress and pain. The curriculum includes:

1. Guided Mindfulness Meditation: Participants are instructed in practices such as body scanning, sitting meditation, and mindful yoga, fostering awareness and acceptance of moment-to-moment experiences.
2. Psychoeducation: Didactic components elucidate the physiology of stress and pain, explicating how mindfulness can disrupt the habitual cycles of psychological distress.
3. Group Dynamics: Collective discussions and exercises foster a supportive milieu, allowing participants to share insights and cultivate a sense of shared humanity.

The Alchemy of MBSR: Transforming Stress into Serenity

The alchemical process of MBSR hinges on the recalibration of our habitual responses to stressors. By nurturing a non-reactive awareness, individuals learn to observe their thoughts, emotions, and bodily sensations without becoming ensnared in them. This mindful stance fosters a space of choice, enabling participants to respond to stressors with greater equanimity and discernment. Empirical studies have substantiated the efficacy of MBSR, demonstrating its capacity to reduce symptoms of anxiety, depression, and chronic pain, while enhancing quality of life and psychological well-being.

MBSR in Contemporary Practice

The influence of MBSR has percolated beyond healthcare, infiltrating domains such as education, corporate wellness, and the criminal justice system. Tailored versions of the program cater to specific populations, addressing the unique stressors and challenges they encounter. Digital platforms have also expanded the reach of MBSR, offering online courses and applications that make the program accessible to a global audience.

In sum, Mindfulness-Based Stress Reduction stands as a testament to the transformative power of mindfulness. By intertwining ancient meditative practices with contemporary psychological insights, MBSR offers a robust, secular approach to mitigating stress and fostering resilience. Its continued evolution and integration into various facets of society underscore the universality and adaptability of mindfulness as a tool for personal and collective well-being.

CHAPTER 21: DEEPENING YOUR MEDITATION PRACTICES

In the preceding chapters of "Noetic Scrying: Divining Through Cognitive States," we have journeyed through the foundational elements of mindfulness and meditation. Now, as we pivot towards deeper realms of self-exploration, Chapter 21 invites us to refine and advance our meditation practices. It's time to transcend the elementary and wade into the waters of intermediate meditation, where stillness, depth, and insight grow more profound.

Advancing from Basic to Intermediate Practices

Transitioning from basic to intermediate meditation practices is akin to a seedling transforming into a sturdy plant. The transition is subtle yet significant, marked by increased duration, depth, and the introduction of more complex techniques. While basic practices are often grounded in the awareness of breath, body, or senses, intermediate techniques involve delving into the layers of the subconscious, harnessing the power of visualization, and embracing the nuances of concentration and insight.

Visualization and Guided Imagery

Visualization is a powerful tool in the meditator's arsenal. It involves conjuring mental images or scenarios that promote peace, healing, or insight. This technique is akin to scrying, using the mind's eye to divine truths from within. Guided imagery, often facilitated by a teacher or recording, leads the practitioner through a series of visualizations to deepen the meditative state, enhance relaxation, and promote emotional healing.

Concentration and Insight Meditation

At the intermediate level, the dichotomy between concentration (Samatha) and insight (Vipassana) meditation becomes more pronounced. Concentration meditation involves focusing intensely on a single point, such as the breath, a mantra, or a candle flame. This unwavering focus quiets the mind and prepares it for deeper states of meditation.

Conversely, insight meditation encourages a broad awareness, observing thoughts, feelings, and sensations without attachment. This practice fosters profound understanding and wisdom, offering a glimpse into the transient nature of reality.

Exploring the Subconscious Mind

As we delve deeper into meditation, we encounter the vast landscape of the subconscious mind. It's a realm brimming with memories, emotions, and insights that often lie beyond the reach of our waking consciousness. Through meditation, we can gently unlock these hidden chambers, bringing light to areas that may need healing or understanding.

Intermediate meditation practices may involve self-inquiry,

exploring questions like "Who am I?" or "What is the nature of my mind?" These questions act as keys, unlocking deeper understanding and self-awareness.

Embracing Silence and Solitude

Silence and solitude become invaluable allies as we deepen our meditation practice. In the absence of external noise, we become acutely aware of the internal symphony. Solitude provides the space necessary for introspection, allowing us to confront and embrace the totality of our being.

Extended silent retreats, often spanning several days or weeks, are a hallmark of intermediate meditation practice. These retreats provide an immersive environment for deep meditation, free from the distractions of daily life.

Integration into Daily Life

Deepening your meditation practice isn't confined to the cushion or the yoga mat; it's about integrating mindfulness and awareness into every aspect of your life. It's the conscious breath taken during a stressful moment at work, the mindful savoring of a meal, or the compassionate awareness in your interactions with others. Meditation becomes less of an activity and more of a way of being.

In Conclusion

Deepening your meditation practice is an invitation to explore the uncharted territories of your mind and spirit. It's a commitment that requires patience, dedication, and a willingness to confront the depths of your being. As you advance in your journey, remember that each step, each breath, and each moment of stillness is a scrying stone, a divinatory tool for self-discovery and transformation.

CHAPTER 22: MINDFULNESS AND QUANTUM THINKING

As we delve into the intricate relationship between mindfulness and the enigmatic realm of quantum mechanics, it becomes apparent that the link between the two is not merely metaphorical but embedded in the very fabric of reality. Quantum thinking, a term that encapsulates the counterintuitive principles of quantum mechanics, invites us to explore the paradoxical nature of reality—where particles can exist in multiple states simultaneously, and observers play an integral role in shaping the outcome of events. In this chapter, we venture into the domain where science and spirituality converge, unwrapping the profound implications of quantum thinking on mindfulness practices.

The Observer Effect: Consciousness and Quantum Mechanics

At the heart of quantum mechanics lies the observer effect, a phenomenon where the act of observation alters the state of a quantum system. This principle suggests that consciousness, the very essence of mindfulness, is not merely a passive witness but an active participant in the fabric of reality. The renowned double-slit experiment, a cornerstone of quantum physics, illustrates how particles behave differently when observed, hinting at a mysterious connection between the observer's consciousness and the observed phenomenon.

In the context of mindfulness, the observer effect takes on a deeper significance. Mindfulness practices cultivate a heightened state of awareness, turning the practitioner into an observer of their own thoughts, emotions, and sensations. This act of observation, akin to the quantum observer effect, can alter the individual's inner reality, leading to profound shifts in perception and experience.

Entanglement and Interconnectedness

Quantum entanglement, another cornerstone of quantum mechanics, reveals that particles can become entwined in such a way that the state of one instantaneously influences the state of another, regardless of the distance separating them. This non-local connection defies the classical notions of space and time, suggesting a fundamental interconnectedness at the quantum level.

Mindfulness practices often emphasize the interconnected nature of all things, encouraging practitioners to cultivate a sense of oneness with the universe. The concept of quantum entanglement resonates deeply with this aspect of mindfulness, providing a scientific framework that supports the experiential realization of interconnectedness achieved through meditative states.

Probability Waves and the Potentiality of Mind

Quantum mechanics introduces the concept of probability waves, where particles exist not as definite entities but as waves of potentiality, collapsing into a particular state only upon observation. This idea parallels the realm of the mind, where thoughts and emotions exist as waves of potential, manifesting into concrete experiences through the lens of our attention and intention.

Mindfulness practices harness the power of focused attention and intention to shape one's cognitive and emotional landscape. By consciously directing the mind's potentiality, individuals can cultivate positive mental states, emotional resilience, and a deeper sense of well-being, mirroring the collapse of probability waves into a chosen reality.

Quantum Superposition and the Multiplicity of Mind

The principle of quantum superposition posits that particles can exist in multiple states simultaneously until observed. This concept echoes the multifaceted nature of the human mind, capable of holding a multitude of thoughts, emotions, and perspectives at any given moment.

Mindfulness teaches us to embrace the complexity of our inner world, acknowledging the coexistence of conflicting thoughts and feelings without judgment. By adopting a stance akin to quantum superposition, practitioners learn to navigate the multilayered landscape of their consciousness, finding harmony amidst the diversity of their mental states.

Conclusion

In exploring the synergy between mindfulness and quantum thinking, we uncover a tapestry woven with threads of science and spirituality, challenging our conventional understanding of reality. The principles of quantum mechanics not only corroborate the experiential insights gained through mindfulness practices but also expand our horizons, inviting us to contemplate the profound implications of consciousness in shaping the very essence of the universe. As we continue our journey through "Noetic Scrying," we carry with us the transformative insights gleaned from the quantum realm, enriching our meditative practices and deepening our connection with the cosmos.

CHAPTER 23: MINDFULNESS AND CREATIVITY

The intricate relationship between mindfulness and creativity is a fascinating conundrum, weaving the threads of consciousness with the vibrant hues of creative expression. This chapter delves into the complex interplay between these two dimensions of the human experience, illuminating how mindfulness can be a catalyst for unleashing the boundless potential of one's creative prowess.

Unleashing Creative Potential Through Mindful Awareness

Mindfulness, in its essence, is the practice of being acutely aware of the present moment without judgment. It's an act of tuning into the nuances of our experiences, thoughts, and emotions. When mindfulness is applied to the creative process, it becomes a powerful tool that can dismantle the barriers to our innate creativity. This synergy between mindfulness and creativity manifests through various avenues.

One such pathway is the diminishment of self-critical thoughts that often inhibit the free flow of creative ideas. By fostering a non-judgmental awareness of one's thoughts, mindfulness allows individuals to observe and dismiss the inner critic that stifles creativity. This opens a vast expanse where ideas can germinate and flourish without the fetters of self-doubt and fear of failure.

Another aspect is the enhancement of divergent thinking, a hallmark of creativity. Divergent thinking is the ability to generate multiple, unique solutions to a problem. Mindfulness cultivates an environment in which the mind is encouraged to wander and explore uncharted territories of thought. This mental exploration is a fertile ground for creative insights and innovative solutions to emerge.

Mindfulness Practices to Spark Creativity

Several mindfulness practices are specifically tailored to nurture the seeds of creativity within us. One such practice is 'mindful observation,' where individuals are encouraged to observe their surroundings with fresh eyes, noticing details and patterns they would typically overlook. This practice heightens sensory awareness and can lead to novel perceptions, a core component of creative thinking.

'Mindful meditation' is another practice that can be transformative. By regularly engaging in meditation, individuals can develop a heightened awareness of their thought patterns, including those that relate to their creative processes. This heightened awareness can lead to a deeper understanding of one's creative blocks and breakthroughs, enabling individuals to navigate their creative journeys with greater insight and clarity.

'Mindful listening' is a practice that involves being fully present and attentive to sounds, whether it's music, nature, or the cacophony of urban life. This form of deep listening can awaken dormant creative ideas and foster a connection with the rhythm and melody inherent in the creative process.

Creativity in Mindfulness Practices

Conversely, creativity also enriches mindfulness practices. Innovative approaches to mindfulness exercises can enhance the experience and make the practice more engaging. For instance, creative visualization during meditation can transform a routine practice into a dynamic journey through one's imagination. Incorporating elements of art, such as drawing or painting, as a form of mindful expression allows for the tangible manifestation of one's inner experiences.

In the context of noetic scrying, the role of creativity is paramount. Noetic scrying is a divinatory practice that relies on deciphering the symbolic language of the subconscious mind. Creativity is the key that unlocks these symbols, transforming them into insights and guidance. Through a creative lens, mindfulness practices become a form of inner alchemy, transmuting the raw material of our thoughts and emotions into golden nuggets of wisdom.

In conclusion, mindfulness and creativity are not just interconnected; they are interdependent, each enriching the other in a symbiotic relationship. Mindfulness provides the fertile soil for creativity to take root and flourish, while creativity infuses mindfulness practices with color, vitality, and innovation. Together, they form a dynamic duo that can lead individuals on a transformative journey of self-discovery and artistic expression. As we advance in our exploration of noetic scrying, the harmonious dance between mindfulness and creativity becomes a pivotal theme, revealing the profound potential that lies within the confluence of these two powerful streams of human consciousness.

CHAPTER 24: TAOIST MEDITATION TECHNIQUES

Taoism, an ancient philosophical and religious tradition rooted in Chinese custom, presents a unique amalgamation of meditation, spirituality, and philosophy. Unlike many traditions, Taoist meditation emphasizes living in harmony with the Tao, or the fundamental principle underlying the universe. This chapter delves into the Taoist approach to meditation, exploring its distinct techniques and the philosophical underpinnings that set it apart from other meditative practices.

The Taoist Philosophy

Taoism encompasses a profound connection with nature and the universe. Central to its belief is the Tao, often translated as 'the Way', which is the source, pattern, and substance of everything that exists. Taoism teaches that humans should align themselves with the Tao to live in harmony and balance. The practice of Taoist meditation, therefore, is not just a technique for relaxation or mindfulness but a means of aligning one's spirit with the cosmic order.

Techniques of Taoist Meditation

Taoist meditation is diverse, with practices ranging from simple breathing exercises to complex visualizations. Here, we explore a few key techniques that embody the essence of Taoist meditative practice.

1. **Zuowang: Sitting in Oblivion**

Zuowang, translating to 'sitting in oblivion', is a form of meditation that encourages practitioners to let go of all thoughts, forms, and images, entering a state of 'emptiness'. It is a practice of forgetting everything and becoming one with the Tao. In this state, the distinction between the self and the universe dissolves, leading to profound peace and insight.

2. **Breathing Techniques**

Breathing is foundational in Taoist meditation, with the belief that breath control can help regulate and enhance the flow of Qi (vital energy) within the body. One common technique is 'embryonic breathing', which involves deep, diaphragmatic breathing to promote relaxation and internal focus. The goal is to breathe as a newborn would, deeply and effortlessly, to foster a sense of purity and connection with the Tao.

3. **Microcosmic Orbit**

This advanced technique involves circulating Qi through two main channels in the body: the Ren and Du meridians. The practitioner visualizes drawing energy up the spine (Du meridian) and down the front of the body (Ren meridian), creating a continuous loop. This practice is said to promote healing, longevity, and spiritual awakening.

Taoist Meditation in Daily Life

Incorporating Taoist meditation into daily life involves more than a set of practices; it's a philosophy that permeates every aspect of existence. Taoism teaches the art of wu-wei, or 'action through non-action', which encourages flowing with life's natural rhythms rather than resisting them. Mindful practices such as walking, Tai Chi, and Qigong are extensions of Taoist meditation, blending movement, breath, and mindfulness in a harmonious whole.

In conclusion, Taoist meditation offers a pathway not only to personal tranquility but to a deeper understanding of the universe and our place within it. By practicing these techniques, individuals can cultivate a profound sense of connection and harmony with the Tao, leading to a balanced and insightful existence.

CHAPTER 25: VIPASSANA MEDITATION

Vipassana, derived from ancient Pali language, literally means "clear seeing" or "insight." It is a meditation technique that aims to cultivate profound self-awareness and insight into the true nature of reality. This chapter delves into the intricacies of Vipassana meditation, its origins, its methodology, and its profound impact on the practitioner's mind and perception.

Origins and Philosophy of Vipassana

Vipassana is one of the oldest meditation practices in India, often attributed to the teachings of Gautama Buddha. It's a cornerstone of Theravada Buddhism but isn't confined to it, extending its influence to various spiritual traditions around the world. The core philosophy of Vipassana is to see things as they truly are, unobscured by our habitual reactions or illusions. It's about observing the continuous interplay of mind and matter, understanding the impermanence of sensations, and ultimately attaining liberation from suffering.

Methodology of Vipassana Meditation

Vipassana is often taught during silent meditation retreats, the most common being 10-day courses. These retreats are intense, requiring participants to adhere to a code of discipline, noble silence, and a rigorous schedule.

1. **Moral Conduct**: Participants start by practicing Sila, the ethical foundation for meditation. This involves abstaining from actions that cause harm, such as lying, stealing, and killing.

2. **Mastery over the Mind**: The next stage is Anapana, focusing on the breath. This practice sharpens concentration, preparing the mind for the deeper work of Vipassana.

3. **Observation and Insight**: Finally, participants practice Vipassana itself. This involves observing sensations throughout the body, understanding their impermanent nature, and not reacting to them. Through this process, one develops insight into the three marks of existence in Buddhism: impermanence (anicca), suffering (dukkha), and non-self (anatta).

Transformative Impact of Vipassana

The transformative potential of Vipassana is vast. By consistently practicing, individuals can peel away layers of conditioned responses and reach a state of equanimity. This equanimity is not indifference but a balanced response to the vicissitudes of life. Practitioners often report reduced stress, enhanced clarity of thought, and a profound sense of peace and contentment. Moreover, the insights gained through Vipassana can have a ripple effect, enhancing compassion and understanding in interpersonal relationships.

In summary, Vipassana meditation is a profound practice that encourages practitioners to see the world as it truly is, free from the distortions of personal bias and emotional reactivity. Through disciplined practice, one can gain deep insights into the nature of reality and one's own mind, leading to a life marked by greater peace, compassion, and wisdom.

CHAPTER 26: THE PSYCHOLOGY OF MINDFULNESS

In the labyrinthine corridors of the human mind, mindfulness acts as a guiding light, illuminating the pathways of our mental processes. As we delve deeper into the intermediate realm of mindfulness, we transcend beyond the basic techniques and rituals to explore the psychological underpinnings that govern the practice. This chapter unveils the symbiotic relationship between mindfulness and psychology, dissecting how they intertwine and influence one another.

Cognitive Architectures and Mindful Awareness

Mindfulness is not just a practice but an inherent part of our cognitive architecture. The human brain is a marvel of evolution, capable of both incredible complexity and profound simplicity. At its core, mindfulness leverages this dual nature of the brain, tapping into the prefrontal cortex, the seat of our higher-order thinking, and the amygdala, the bastion of our emotions. Through mindful practices, we forge a bridge between these two, tempering the fiery impulses of the amygdala with the reasoned calm of the prefrontal cortex. This neural handshake leads to enhanced emotional regulation, heightened awareness, and a richer tapestry of cognitive functioning.

Psychological Theories in the Landscape of Mindfulness

Several psychological theories intersect with mindfulness, providing a framework for understanding its effects. The constructivist theory posits that individuals construct their reality based on their experiences and beliefs. Mindfulness, by encouraging non-judgmental awareness, allows for a more flexible and adaptive construction of reality, one that is less tethered to preconceived notions and biases.

Flow theory, on the other hand, speaks of a state where individuals are fully immersed and engaged in activities, leading to a sense of joy and fulfillment. Mindfulness practices nurture this state of flow by honing focus and reducing the cacophony of distractions that often besiege our minds.

Lastly, the stress-buffering theory elucidates how mindfulness can serve as a protective barrier against stress. By fostering a calm and centered mind, mindfulness practices enable individuals to better withstand the vicissitudes of stress, thereby promoting a state of mental resilience.

Mindfulness and Psychological Pathologies

Mindfulness has been a beacon of hope in the realm of psychological pathologies. Its utility in clinical psychology is not just a testament to its versatility but also to its profound impact on mental health. Mindfulness-Based Cognitive Therapy (MBCT), for instance, has emerged as a potent intervention for depression, preventing relapse by teaching individuals to disengage from the habitual patterns of negative thinking that often precipitate a depressive episode.

Similarly, in the domain of anxiety disorders, mindfulness helps to anchor the mind in the present moment, curtailing the tendency to catastrophize about the future. This shift from a future-oriented worry to a present-oriented awareness can be transformative for those ensnared by anxiety's grip.

The intersection of mindfulness and psychology is a landscape rich with insights and discoveries. As we continue our journey through the chapters of this book, we delve deeper into the cognitive realms, unearthing the multifaceted ways in which mindfulness not only shapes our mental processes but also illuminates the contours of our inner world. Mindfulness, with its roots firmly planted in the fertile soil of psychology, continues to grow and evolve, offering a beacon of hope and understanding in the intricate dance of the human mind.

CHAPTER 27: SELF-COMPASSION IN MINDFULNESS

In the intricate tapestry of mindfulness, the thread of self-compassion weaves a pattern of profound significance. This chapter delves into the symbiotic relationship between mindfulness and self-compassion, exploring how the cultivation of a compassionate attitude towards oneself can enhance mindfulness practices and contribute to an enriched life experience.

The Essence of Self-Compassion

Self-compassion, at its core, is the art of being kind and understanding towards oneself in instances of pain or failure, rather than being harshly self-critical. It entails recognizing that imperfection and suffering are universal human experiences. Dr. Kristin Neff, a pioneering researcher in the field, conceptualizes self-compassion as comprising three main components: self-kindness, common humanity, and mindfulness. These elements create a nurturing environment for personal growth and emotional resilience.

Interplay Between Mindfulness and Self-Compassion

Mindfulness, the practice of maintaining a moment-by-moment awareness of our thoughts, feelings, bodily sensations, and surrounding environment, offers a nonjudgmental space. It is within this space that self-compassion flourishes. Mindfulness provides the awareness necessary to recognize when one is suffering, while self-compassion provides the warm, supportive response. This symbiosis not only alleviates personal distress but also motivates constructive, healthy behaviors.

Research illustrates that mindfulness and self-compassion synergistically enhance well-being. For instance, individuals with higher levels of self-compassion tend to experience less anxiety and depression. They exhibit a greater capacity for emotional regulation, demonstrating an ability to soothe themselves when upset. Furthermore, the practice of self-compassion can be especially beneficial in silencing the often debilitating inner critic, replacing self-criticism with supportive inner dialogue.

Cultivating Self-Compassion through Mindfulness

Developing self-compassion can be a transformative journey. Mindfulness practices provide fertile ground for this development. One foundational exercise is the 'Self-Compassion Break', a technique designed to foster compassionate responses. The practice involves three steps: acknowledging suffering, recognizing common humanity, and offering kindness to oneself. It can be incorporated into daily life, providing immediate comfort and long-term nurturing.

Another technique is 'Loving-Kindness Meditation' (LKM), which traditionally begins with the self before extending compassion outward. LKM enhances positive emotions and encourages a compassionate attitude, both towards oneself and others. Additionally, 'Mindful Self-Compassion' (MSC), an empirically-supported program, combines the skills of mindfulness and self-compassion to promote emotional well-being. These practices exemplify how mindfulness can serve as a crucible for cultivating self-compassion.

Self-Compassion in the Noetic Realm

In the context of noetic scrying, self-compassion can be a powerful ally. As one delves into the depths of the psyche and navigates the nuanced terrains of cognitive states, self-compassion provides a nurturing touchstone. It fosters an attitude of kindness and patience towards oneself during the exploratory process. This compassionate stance enhances the introspective journey, allowing for a more profound and benevolent engagement with one's inner world.

In summary, self-compassion is an indispensable facet of mindfulness. It enriches the practice by introducing a heart-centered approach to personal challenges and adversities. Through the thoughtful integration of self-compassion into mindfulness practices, individuals can unlock deeper levels of emotional healing, well-being, and self-discovery. As we advance in our understanding and application of mindfulness, the cultivation of self-compassion remains a beacon of kindness, guiding us towards a more empathetic and harmonious existence.

CHAPTER 28: THERAVADA MEDITATION PRACTICES

In the rich tapestry of meditation traditions, Theravada Buddhism presents itself as one of the most ancient and methodically preserved practices. Originating from the Pali canon, the oldest recorded teachings of the Buddha, Theravada meditation practices have transcended centuries, offering a wellspring of wisdom and technique for the contemporary seeker. As we delve into the intricate patterns and profound depths of Theravada meditation, let us explore its foundational principles, core practices, and the transformative impact it promises for the earnest practitioner.

Foundational Principles of Theravada Meditation

At the heart of Theravada meditation lies the unwavering pursuit of enlightenment or 'Nibbana' — a state beyond all suffering, defilements, and the cycle of rebirth. Theravada, often translated as the "Teaching of the Elders," is grounded in the Pali scriptures known as the Tipitaka, which systematically chronicle the Buddha's discourses, moral codes, and the monastic way of life.

Central to these teachings is the Noble Eightfold Path, encompassing wisdom (right understanding and right thought), ethical conduct (right speech, right action, and right livelihood), and mental discipline (right effort, right mindfulness, and right concentration). It is within this framework of mental discipline that Theravada meditation blossoms, guiding the meditator through the intricacies of mind and phenomena.

Core Practices of Theravada Meditation

Theravada meditation can be broadly categorized into two primary practices: Samatha (tranquility meditation) and Vipassana (insight meditation). While distinct in approach, both practices are interwoven and often complement each other in a practitioner's journey.

Samatha Meditation: Samatha meditation focuses on developing concentration and tranquility, preparing the mind for deeper insight. It often involves the practice of 'Anapanasati' — mindful breathing — where attention is gently anchored to the breath, fostering a state of calm and collectedness. As the mind settles, it becomes a fertile ground for the cultivation of 'Jhana' — absorptive states of deep concentration characterized by profound peace and joy.

Vipassana Meditation: Vipassana, on the other hand, emphasizes direct, experiential understanding of the nature of reality. It involves keen observation of bodily sensations, mental formations, and phenomena, cultivating insights into the Three Marks of Existence — impermanence (anicca), suffering (dukkha), and non-self (anatta). The Mahasi Sayadaw technique and the Goenka method are contemporary adaptations of Vipassana that have gained international recognition, fostering mindfulness through systematic noting and body scanning techniques.

Transformative Impact of Theravada Meditation

The diligent practice of Theravada meditation techniques gradually dissolves layers of ignorance and delusion, revealing the impermanent and interdependent nature of all phenomena. This insight into 'anicca' and 'anatta' leads to a profound shift in perspective, diminishing the grip of craving and aversion that fuels the cyclic existence of 'samsara'.

As practitioners advance in their journey, they encounter the transformative stages of 'sotapatti' (stream-entry), 'sakadagami' (once-returner), 'anagami' (non-returner), and ultimately 'arahantship' — the pinnacle of spiritual liberation in Theravada Buddhism. It is a path that demands unwavering dedication, ethical purity, and meditative rigor.

Conclusion

Theravada meditation practices offer a venerable and well-trodden path to self-discovery and enlightenment. Grounded in the ancient wisdom of the Buddha's teachings, they beckon the modern practitioner to embark on a journey of introspection, mindfulness, and ultimate liberation. Whether one seeks tranquility, insight, or the profound liberation of Nibbana, Theravada meditation stands as a testament to the enduring power of mindfulness and the potential for transformation within us all.

CHAPTER 29: COGNITIVE DISSONANCE AND MINDFULNESS

Cognitive dissonance, a term coined by the psychologist Leon Festinger in the 1950s, refers to the psychological discomfort that arises from holding two contradictory beliefs, values, or attitudes. This dissonance is not merely an academic notion; it permeates our daily lives, shaping our reactions, decisions, and, ultimately, our sense of self. Mindfulness, with its roots firmly planted in the fertile soil of introspective practices, offers a unique lens through which to view and address the discord of cognitive dissonance. This chapter delves into the interplay between these two facets of human psychology, exploring how mindfulness can be a tool for recognizing, understanding, and reconciling cognitive dissonance.

Mindfulness: An Antidote to Dissonance

The principle of mindfulness, grounded in non-judgmental awareness and acceptance, stands in stark contrast to the tension generated by cognitive dissonance. When we cultivate mindfulness, we learn to observe our thoughts and feelings without immediately reacting to them or trying to alter them.

This observational stance provides a buffer against the knee-jerk impulse to resolve dissonance by adjusting our beliefs or denying information that conflicts with them. By fostering a state of openness and curiosity, mindfulness can diminish the need to immediately resolve dissonance and instead encourage a more thoughtful, coherent integration of conflicting information.

Cognitive Dissonance in Everyday Life

Cognitive dissonance is not a rare psychological phenomenon encountered only in extreme situations. It is woven into the fabric of everyday life. Whether it's a simple act of purchasing an item we don't need or espousing an environmental ethic while driving a fuel-inefficient vehicle, dissonance is ubiquitous. The mindfulness approach, in this context, invites us to observe these contradictions without immediate self-critique. This observational pause can reveal the deeper values and beliefs that underpin our actions, providing a clearer path to align our behaviors with our genuine convictions.

Mindfulness Practices for Reconciling Dissonance

The chapter would be incomplete without providing readers with tangible practices to apply mindfulness to cognitive dissonance. Here are a few techniques:

- **Observational Journaling**: Keeping a journal to record instances of dissonance can provide clarity. Writing down conflicting beliefs and the emotions they evoke creates distance, allowing for a more objective assessment.
- **Mindful Inquiry**: This involves asking oneself probing questions during meditation. For instance, "Why does

this dissonance arise?" or "What values are in conflict here?" Such questions, asked in a state of meditative calm, can yield profound insights.

- **Compassionate Acceptance**: Learning to accept the presence of dissonance without self-critique is pivotal. Mindfulness encourages us to approach our internal conflicts with compassion, acknowledging them as part of the human experience.

In conclusion, this chapter does not promise an easy resolution to the complexity of cognitive dissonance. Instead, it proposes mindfulness as a means of navigating the tumultuous waters of contradictory beliefs and values. Through mindful observation, inquiry, and acceptance, we can approach dissonance not as a problem to be swiftly resolved but as an opportunity for deeper self-understanding and growth.

CHAPTER 30: MINDFULNESS IN DAILY ROUTINES

Embedding Mindfulness into the Fabric of Daily Life

In the rush and bustle of modern life, it's easy to lose touch with the present moment. The mind often dwells in the past or frets about the future, leaving little space for the richness of the 'now'. But what if we could weave mindfulness seamlessly into our daily routines, transforming mundane tasks into moments of deep presence and awareness?

Mindfulness isn't confined to the cushion or the yoga mat. It's a portable practice, one that can be integrated into all aspects of life. By inviting mindfulness into our daily routines, we cultivate a continuous thread of awareness, turning the ordinary into the extraordinary.

The Alchemy of Routine Tasks

Routine tasks—brushing teeth, washing dishes, commuting—are often performed on autopilot, with our minds wandering elsewhere. But these moments are opportunities for practice, arenas in which mindfulness can be cultivated. When brushing your teeth, for example, instead of letting your mind roam, focus on the sensations: the taste of the toothpaste, the sound of the bristles, the rhythm of your hand movements. Such simple acts become rituals of presence, imbuing the ordinary with a sense of the sacred.

Mindfulness and Productivity

In the workplace, mindfulness can enhance productivity and creativity. It's not about working more hours, but about working more mindfully. By being fully present with each task, we work more efficiently, make fewer errors, and come up with more innovative solutions. Mindful breaks, even if just for a few breaths, can reinvigorate the mind and body, leading to greater effectiveness throughout the workday.

Cultivating Mindful Relationships

Mindfulness can also transform our interactions with others. In conversations, practicing mindful listening—giving someone your full attention without formulating your response while they're speaking—deepens connections and fosters understanding. Mindful communication involves being aware of not only what you say but also how you say it, noticing your tone, body language, and underlying emotions. Through mindful presence, relationships become richer, imbued with greater empathy and compassion.

In Summary

Incorporating mindfulness into daily routines doesn't require additional time; it's about shifting how we engage with the moments already present in our lives. By transforming routine tasks into opportunities for practice, enhancing productivity with presence, and enriching our relationships through mindful interactions, we infuse each day with a deeper sense of meaning and connection. Mindfulness, when woven into the fabric of daily life, reveals the profound in the mundane and illuminates the extraordinary nature of the ordinary.

CHAPTER 31: MINDFULNESS AND SOCIAL RELATIONSHIPS

The intricate web of human relationships, a complex tapestry of emotions, expectations, and interactions, is an area where mindfulness can play a particularly transformative role. The essence of mindfulness, with its emphasis on presence and awareness, provides a unique lens through which to view and improve our social relationships. This chapter delves into the profound ways in which mindfulness can enrich interpersonal connections, helping to foster understanding, empathy, and stronger bonds.

The Reflective Mirror of Mindfulness in Communication

Communication is the cornerstone of any relationship, and mindfulness can act as a reflective mirror, enhancing our interactions with others. By being fully present, we can truly listen, not just with the intent to reply but to understand. This attentive presence allows for a deeper connection, reducing misunderstandings and fostering a sense of being heard and valued. Moreover, mindfulness helps in regulating our emotional responses. It gives us the space to pause and choose our reactions, rather than being swept away by impulsive emotions. This is particularly beneficial in managing conflicts, where mindful communication can de-escalate tensions and lead to more constructive resolutions.

Empathy and Compassion: Heart of Mindful Relationships

Empathy and compassion are natural by-products of a mindful approach to relationships. When we are present and truly attuned to the experiences of others, our capacity for empathy grows. We become better at understanding their perspectives, feelings, and needs. This empathic resonance can bridge divides and create a sense of shared humanity. Compassion follows empathy, as understanding naturally leads to a desire to alleviate suffering. In practicing mindfulness, we nurture a compassionate heart that is responsive and caring, profoundly influencing our social interactions in a positive way.

Interconnectedness and Mindful Interactions

At its core, mindfulness reveals the interconnectedness of all beings. This recognition of interdependence fosters a sense of belonging and can transform our social relationships. When we see ourselves in others and recognize our shared human experience, our interactions become more genuine and meaningful. This interconnectedness encourages us to act with kindness and consideration, knowing that our actions have ripple effects in the web of relationships. Mindfulness thus becomes a vehicle for nurturing a more compassionate and interconnected society.

In conclusion, incorporating mindfulness into our social relationships can lead to profound changes. It enhances communication, fosters empathy and compassion, and reveals the interconnectedness that binds us all. By bringing mindful presence into our interactions, we open the door to deeper, more meaningful connections that enrich not only our lives but also the lives of those around us.

CHAPTER 32: DREAM YOGA AND LUCID DREAMING

Dream Yoga and Lucid Dreaming represent profound aspects of mindfulness practices, offering an enigmatic journey into the nocturnal aspects of our consciousness. This chapter delves into the mystical intersection where dreams become a playground for mindfulness, a realm traditionally explored within the Tibetan practice of Dream Yoga and the modern understanding of lucid dreaming. Both these practices offer a unique perspective on the mind's capabilities and its malleable nature during sleep.

Dream Yoga: An Ancient Tibetan Practice

Dream Yoga, a practice that originates from Tibetan Buddhism, is an intricate method of harnessing the dream state to achieve spiritual awakening. This practice is more than mere dream control; it's a form of meditation performed while dreaming. According to ancient Tibetan beliefs, Dream Yoga facilitates a deep understanding of the illusory nature of reality, both in the dream state and in waking life. Practitioners of Dream Yoga engage in a series of progressive exercises that help them recognize the dream as a dream, dissolve the fears and limitations within it, and eventually, gain the ability to transform the dream environment at will. By mastering these techniques, the dreamer can embark on profound spiritual journeys, encountering symbolic representations of their subconscious mind and spiritual guides.

Lucid Dreaming: A Modern Exploration

In contrast, Lucid Dreaming is a term that has been popularized in the West and refers to the phenomenon where an individual becomes aware that they are dreaming while still immersed in the dream. This awareness can range from a faint recognition of the dream state to a powerful and vivid awakening within the dream world. Once lucidity is achieved, the dreamer can exert varying degrees of control over their dream environment, characters, and narrative. The psychological implications of lucid dreaming are immense, as it offers a direct window into the subconscious, allowing for explorations of deep-seated fears, aspirations, and suppressed memories. Furthermore, lucid dreaming has been utilized as a therapeutic tool, aiding in the treatment of nightmares, enhancing creative problem-solving, and even serving as a rehearsal space for real-life situations.

Intersecting Pathways: Mindfulness in Dreams

Both Dream Yoga and Lucid Dreaming share common ground in their use of mindfulness within the dream state. Mindfulness, the state of active, open attention to the present moment, becomes a tool for recognizing and maintaining lucidity. The same principles that apply to mindfulness during waking hours — observation without judgment, presence, and conscious awareness — become pivotal in maintaining lucidity in dreams. Through mindfulness, the dreamer learns to navigate the dream with a sense of clarity and purpose, transcending the chaotic and random nature of typical dream narratives.

Practicing mindfulness within dreams is not only fascinating but can also have profound implications for personal growth and spiritual development. It encourages a deeper connection with the subconscious mind, fostering an understanding of inner desires, fears, and patterns of thought that often escape conscious recognition. Moreover, it enhances one's ability to remain present and composed in the face of unpredictability, a skill that undoubtedly transfers to waking life challenges.

As we conclude this chapter, we are reminded that the realms of sleep and dreams offer untapped potential for mindfulness practice. Whether through the ancient traditions of Dream Yoga or the contemporary explorations of lucid dreaming, these nocturnal practices present a unique pathway towards self-discovery and cognitive enrichment. They represent a frontier where mindfulness transcends the constraints of the waking state, opening doors to profound spiritual and psychological insights.

CHAPTER 33: ESOTERIC TRADITIONS IN MINDFULNESS

As we venture deeper into the multifaceted realm of mindfulness, it's imperative to recognize that this practice isn't merely a contemporary phenomenon or a modern trend. Its roots are entwined with the esoteric and mystical traditions of antiquity, where the pursuit of inner knowledge and universal truths was as much a spiritual endeavor as it was a mental exercise. This chapter delves into the enigmatic aspects of mindfulness, unraveling its connections to ancient wisdom and esoteric practices.

The Tapestry of Mystical Traditions

At the heart of many esoteric traditions lies the pursuit of gnosis - a form of deep, intuitive knowledge of spiritual truths. This quest often manifests in practices designed to transcend ordinary consciousness and attain a state of enlightenment or spiritual awakening. Mindfulness, in its deepest essence, is akin to these pursuits. It isn't merely about being present in the moment; it's about piercing the veil of mundane reality to glimpse the profound interconnectedness of all things.

From the mystics of the Kabbalah who meditated on the divine emanations of the Tree of Life, to the Sufis whose whirling dances were a form of moving meditation aimed at union with the divine, mindfulness has been a cornerstone of esoteric practices. In these traditions, mindfulness wasn't just a method of mental discipline but a pathway to the sacred, a means of aligning the individual soul with the cosmic rhythm.

Alchemy of the Mind

Alchemy, often misconceived as merely the transmutation of base metals into gold, is intrinsically linked with transformative mental practices. The alchemists' Magnum Opus or Great Work was as much about spiritual purification and enlightenment as it was about physical substances. Mindfulness in this context can be seen as the mental crucible within which base thoughts are transmuted into the gold of higher consciousness.

Meditative techniques akin to mindfulness were employed by alchemists to focus their minds and attune their inner vibrations with the universal energy they believed was essential for their work. Through these practices, they sought to refine their souls, turning the leaden weight of earthly concerns into the gold of spiritual awakening.

The Hermetic Corpus and Thrice-Great Hermes

In the hermetic tradition, attributed to Hermes Trismegistus, a legendary Hellenistic figure who was a syncretism of the Greek god Hermes and the Egyptian god Thoth, mindfulness takes on a metaphysical dimension. The Hermetic Corpus, a collection of texts central to this tradition, emphasizes the importance of mastering one's mental state to perceive the underlying unity of the cosmos.

The hermetic axiom "As above, so below; as within, so without" encapsulates the essence of mindfulness in esoteric practices. It implies that by cultivating inner awareness and harmony, one can align with the macrocosm, understanding the universe not only intellectually but experientially.

Mindfulness in Gnosticism

Gnosticism, a collection of ancient religious ideas and systems, also has significant overlap with the principles of mindfulness. Gnostic texts often speak of the importance of self-awareness and inner knowledge as tools to comprehend the divine spark within. They teach that through introspective mindfulness, one can peel away the layers of illusion that shroud the true spiritual nature of reality.

For the Gnostics, salvation was found not through dogma or ritual but through an experiential understanding of one's divine essence. Mindfulness practices, therefore, were crucial for this inner revelation, acting as a catalyst for the recognition of one's own divinity and the illusionary nature of material existence.

Integrating Esoteric Mindfulness into Modern Practices

While the context of these esoteric traditions may differ significantly from contemporary mindfulness practices, the core principles remain remarkably consistent. Both seek to transcend the ordinary, to touch upon a reality that lies beyond the confines of the mundane. As practitioners of mindfulness in the modern age, there is much to be learned from these ancient traditions.

By incorporating elements of esoteric mindfulness into our practices, we can deepen our understanding of what it means to be truly present. It's not simply about calming the mind or reducing stress; it's about connecting with something greater, a universal truth that has echoed through the ages in the teachings of mystics, alchemists, and gnostics alike.

In this advanced stage of our exploration, we see that mindfulness isn't just a tool for personal development; it's a bridge to the mystical, a path trodden by seekers of truth across centuries. As we continue our journey through noetic scrying, let us carry with us the wisdom of these esoteric traditions, allowing it to illuminate our path toward deeper understanding and spiritual fulfillment.

CHAPTER 34: MINDFULNESS AND NON-DUAL AWARENESS

In the intricate labyrinth of cognitive exploration, the concept of non-dual awareness stands as a beacon, illuminating the depths of mindfulness practices. This chapter delves into the realm of non-dualistic philosophies, a domain where the binary oppositions of self and other, observer and observed, dissolve into a seamless unity. Here, mindfulness is not just a practice but a state of being, an ontological stance that redefines the contours of consciousness.

The Non-Dual Perspective: An Overview

Non-dualism, a term rooted in Eastern philosophical traditions, notably Advaita Vedanta and Buddhism, refers to a state of consciousness where the dichotomy between subject and object ceases to exist. It's a perspective where the illusion of a separate self is transcended, and one experiences the reality as an undifferentiated whole. Mindfulness, in its most profound form, can be a gateway to this non-dual awareness, offering insights into the interconnectedness of all phenomena.

Mindfulness Practices and Non-Dual Consciousness

In the realm of mindfulness, non-dual awareness can be approached through various practices designed to dissolve the ego-centric perspective. These practices entail an acute attentiveness to the present moment, a surrendering of judgment, and an embrace of the totality of experience.

1. **Meditative Absorption**: Certain meditative states, known as 'Jhanas' in the Buddhist tradition, encourage a deep absorption in the object of meditation. This immersion blurs the boundaries between the meditator and the meditated upon, fostering a non-dual consciousness.

2. **Open Awareness Meditation**: Unlike focused meditation, open awareness involves widening the lens of attention to include all sensations, thoughts, and feelings without clinging to any. This expansiveness can cultivate a sense of oneness with the environment.

3. **Self-Inquiry**: Popularized by the sage Ramana Maharshi, the method of self-inquiry involves persistent questioning of the nature of the 'I' or self. This relentless introspection can lead to the realization that the true self is not the limited ego but an expansive, non-dual awareness.

The Science Behind Non-Dual Awareness

In recent times, neuroscientific studies have ventured into understanding non-dual awareness, investigating its correlates in the brain. Research utilizing functional magnetic resonance imaging (fMRI) and electroencephalography (EEG) suggests that non-dual awareness is associated with decreased activity in the default mode network (DMN), a brain network implicated in self-referential thoughts and the construction of the ego. The quieting of this network aligns with the experiential reports of non-dual practitioners who describe a dissolution of the sense of self.

Non-Dual Awareness in Everyday Life

Non-dual awareness need not be confined to the cushions of meditation. It can permeate one's daily life, transforming mundane activities into portals of transcendence. Practicing mindfulness with a non-dual attitude involves seeing the interconnectedness in everyday occurrences, recognizing oneself in others, and dismantling the habitual patterns of reactivity that reinforce a sense of separateness.

In summary, the journey into non-dual awareness through mindfulness is not about acquiring something new but about recognizing what has always been present. It's a radical shift in perspective, a profound realization that the separation between self and other is but a delusion. This chapter has ventured to explore this enigmatic state of consciousness, offering insights and practices to those seekers inclined towards unraveling the tapestry of non-duality.

CHAPTER 35: ADVANCED SENSORY PERCEPTION TECHNIQUES

In the expansive domain of mindfulness, our senses serve as portals to the present moment, anchors to the here and now. As we delve into Chapter 35 of "Noetic Scrying: Divining Through Cognitive States," we embark on a journey to heighten our sensory perception through advanced mindfulness techniques. This chapter unfurls the tapestry of advanced practices that go beyond mere observation, venturing into the realms of augmentation and profound sensory engagement.

1. Synesthetic Meditation Practices

Synesthesia, a neurological condition where stimulation of one sensory pathway leads to involuntary experiences in another sensory pathway, has been a source of fascination in both scientific and mindfulness communities. Although typically a naturally occurring phenomenon, there's a burgeoning interest in adopting synesthetic principles into meditation practices.

In these advanced sensory perception techniques, practitioners engage in exercises designed to blend senses deliberately. For example, they may focus on the sound of a bell and visualize the reverberations as tangible waves of color or texture. Over time, such exercises are not only posited to enhance mindfulness but also cultivate a more rich, interconnected experience of the sensory world.

2. Sensory Deprivation and Heightened Awareness

At the other end of the spectrum lies the practice of sensory deprivation, a technique often employed in advanced mindfulness circles to amplify the remaining senses. This can be achieved through various means, from silent retreats and darkened meditation spaces to more contemporary approaches such as floatation tanks, where practitioners are suspended in a saltwater solution in complete darkness and silence.

The deprivation of external stimuli is said to heighten internal awareness dramatically. Practitioners report intensified inner experiences, from vivid visualizations to profound insights. This deep dive into the internal sensory world can lead to a greater understanding of the mind's workings and, subsequently, a more nuanced experience of the external sensory world when returning from such states of sensory absence.

3. Mindful Multisensory Integration

The integration of multiple senses in mindfulness practices embodies a holistic approach to perception. Advanced mindfulness practitioners often engage in exercises designed to harmonize and enhance the interplay between senses. This can involve synchronized practices such as walking meditations, where the touch, sight, and sound of each step are experienced in a concerted fashion, or more complex rituals that engage all senses simultaneously.

The goal of multisensory integration is to create a more

immersive and totalizing experience of the present moment, one that transcends the sum of its parts. By bringing awareness to the synergistic interplay between senses, practitioners aim to cultivate a deeper, more visceral understanding of their moment-to-moment experience.

As we conclude this exploration of advanced sensory perception techniques in mindfulness, it is evident that these practices serve to deepen our connection to the sensory world, amplify our present-moment awareness, and ultimately, enhance our overall experience of consciousness. Engaging in synesthetic meditation, sensory deprivation, and mindful multisensory integration offers a kaleidoscopic view of our sensory capabilities, propelling us into a more profound, richly textured experience of being.

CHAPTER 36: KUNDALINI AND ENERGY WORK

The esoteric doctrines of the East have long posited that within every individual lies a dormant power, a coiled serpent waiting to ascend. This chapter delves into the profound realms of Kundalini, a concept in yogic philosophy that represents a primal energy at the base of the spine. In the context of advanced meditation practices, Kundalini is more than a metaphor; it embodies the potential for transcendental awakening and the unification of consciousness with the divine.

Unraveling the Kundalini Mystery

Kundalini, often depicted as a serpent coiled three and a half times, resides at the base of the spine in the Muladhara chakra, the root energy center. According to yogic traditions, awakening the Kundalini isn't a trivial pursuit; it's a transformative journey that catalyzes profound shifts in perception, consciousness, and the energetic body. This awakening is akin to an energetic symphony where the serpentine power ascends through the Sushumna Nadi, the central energy channel, activating the chakras and culminating at the Sahasrara, the crown chakra, symbolizing the union with the cosmic consciousness.

The Mechanics of Kundalini Activation

Activating the Kundalini energy is an intricate process, one that demands dedication, understanding, and often, the guidance of an adept guru. It involves a series of physical postures (asanas), breath control (pranayama), mudras (hand gestures), and mantras (sacred sounds), all orchestrated towards awakening and guiding the Kundalini energy. The practice of Kundalini yoga, a form synthesized for this very purpose, emphasizes the need for a holistic approach combining these elements.

As the Kundalini ascends, practitioners often report experiencing intense heat, profound visions, or overwhelming emotions. This phenomenon, known as a Kundalini awakening, can be a double-edged sword. When guided and managed properly, it can lead to unparalleled spiritual growth. However, if mismanaged or forced, it can result in what's known as Kundalini syndrome, a constellation of physical and psychological disturbances.

Kundalini in the Context of Modern Mindfulness

In contemporary mindfulness practices, Kundalini is viewed not just as a spiritual endeavor but also as a transformative psychological process. It is increasingly studied in the context of its impact on mental health, self-awareness, and emotional regulation. The awakening is seen as a profound psychological rebirth, shedding the layers of the ego and unveiling the authentic self.

Moreover, the energy work involved in Kundalini practices aligns with the principles of noetic scrying. As practitioners cultivate a deeper awareness of their internal energy flows, they often report heightened intuitive abilities and an enhanced sense of connection with the world around them. The disciplined focus required to navigate Kundalini's potent energy fosters a profound mindfulness that resonates with the divinatory aspects of noetic scrying.

In summary, Kundalini and energy work represent a pinnacle in the journey of mindfulness and meditation. They serve as gateways to exploring the depths of consciousness and unlocking potentials that lie dormant within. This chapter serves as a primer to the enigmatic and transformative world of Kundalini, offering a glimpse into the profound shifts in consciousness that await those who dare to tread this path.

CHAPTER 37: CONSCIOUSNESS ALTERING SUBSTANCES AND MINDFULNESS

Delving into the depths of consciousness, this chapter explores the intersection of mindfulness with consciousness-altering substances. In an age where the quest for inner peace and cognitive expansion treads new paths, we find the fusion of ancient mindfulness practices with modern psychonautics to be both intriguing and complex. The use of such substances, ranging from plant-based psychedelics to synthetic compounds, has raised profound questions about the nature of consciousness, the potential for therapeutic applications, and the ethical considerations that accompany their use.

Psychedelics and Mindful Expansion

Psychedelics, a class of psychoactive substances that induce profound changes in perception, mood, and thought, have a long-standing history with human consciousness exploration. These substances, including psilocybin (found in magic mushrooms), LSD, and ayahuasca (a brew from the Amazon), are known for their ability to dissolve the ego and foster a sense of interconnectedness with the universe—a state often sought in advanced mindfulness practices.

Recent scientific research has revitalized interest in the therapeutic potential of psychedelics. Clinical studies have shown promising results in treating conditions such as depression, anxiety, and PTSD. This has sparked a dialogue on the role of these substances in catalyzing mindful awareness and fostering deep personal transformation. When used responsibly and in controlled settings, psychedelics can act as catalysts, propelling individuals into heightened states of mindfulness that might otherwise take years of disciplined practice to achieve.

Entheogens and Spiritual Mindfulness

Entheogens, a term that means "generating the divine within", refers to substances that are used in a spiritual or religious context to elicit mystical experiences. Traditional cultures across the globe have incorporated entheogens such as peyote, iboga, and ayahuasca into their spiritual practices for centuries. These substances are revered for their ability to impart wisdom, connect individuals with the divine, and provide healing.

The confluence of entheogens and mindfulness in spiritual practices can provide profound insights into the nature of the self and the universe. The intentional use of these substances, often within ceremonial contexts, can facilitate deep states of meditation, foster a sense of oneness, and lead to transformative insights that align with the core principles of mindfulness.

Ethical Considerations and Mindful Use

The use of consciousness-altering substances is not without controversy. It raises ethical questions about consent, the potential for abuse, and the commodification of traditional practices. The mindful use of these substances necessitates an approach grounded in respect, intentionality, and responsibility. It calls for the integration of set (mindset) and setting (environment) to ensure a safe and beneficial experience.

Legal frameworks around the world vary significantly, with some countries and regions decriminalizing or even legalizing certain substances for therapeutic or religious use. This ongoing legal evolution reflects a growing acknowledgment of the potential benefits these substances hold when used mindfully and with reverence.

Integration of Experiences

A crucial aspect of combining mindfulness with consciousness-altering substances is the integration of the experiences they elicit. Profound psychedelic experiences can be overwhelming and challenging to decipher. Mindfulness practices provide the tools to process, understand, and integrate these experiences into one's life. Techniques such as meditation, journaling, and mindful reflection can help individuals extract meaning from their experiences and apply the insights gained in their daily lives.

In conclusion, the interplay between mindfulness and consciousness-altering substances opens up new frontiers in understanding the human psyche. It beckons us to explore the transformative potential of these substances when used with intention, respect, and a mindful approach. As we continue to unravel the mysteries of consciousness, the convergence of ancient wisdom with modern psychonautics offers a unique lens through which we can expand our cognitive horizons and foster deeper connections with ourselves and the world around us.

CHAPTER 38: MINDFULNESS AND META-ETHICS

The exploration of mindfulness, with its many facets, opens up a profound discourse on the ethical dimensions of human experience. The practice of mindfulness is not just an exercise in mental acuity or emotional regulation; it becomes a fulcrum upon which the levers of ethical considerations pivot. This chapter delves into the meta-ethical implications of mindfulness, unveiling how this practice influences our moral philosophy and ethical behavior.

Ethical Awareness in Mindfulness

Mindfulness, by its very nature, entails a heightened state of awareness. This awareness is not just confined to one's thoughts, emotions, or sensations; it extends to the realm of ethical perception. Mindfulness cultivates a discerning awareness that becomes finely attuned to the nuances of right and wrong, good and bad. Practitioners often report an increased sensitivity to ethical dilemmas, a clearer understanding of their personal values, and a stronger inclination toward ethical behavior.

Meta-Ethical Reflections

Meta-ethics, in its exploration of the nature of morality, raises questions about the origins and meanings of ethical principles. It is here that mindfulness intersects with this philosophical domain, offering insights into the subjective experience of ethical understanding. Mindfulness can influence meta-ethical positions in several ways:

1. **Moral Relativism versus Moral Absolutism:** Through mindfulness, one might come to recognize the fluidity and context-dependence of certain moral judgments, potentially aligning more with moral relativism. Conversely, mindfulness may also reveal to some a deeper, perhaps universal, moral truth that aligns with moral absolutism.

2. **Moral Cognitivism versus Non-Cognitivism:** Does mindfulness lead to moral cognitivism, where ethical statements are expressions of beliefs that can be true or false? Or does it lead to non-cognitivism, where ethical statements are merely expressions of emotional reactions or prescriptions that cannot be true or false? The mindful examination of one's ethical reactions and the intentions behind them can provide insights into this dichotomy.

3. **Moral Motivation:** Mindfulness also sheds light on the motivational aspects of ethics. It raises questions about what motivates moral behavior. Is it a pursuit of eudaimonia, a sense of duty, or something else? Mindfulness helps practitioners introspect on their ethical drives, examining whether their motivations are altruistic, egoistic, or a blend of various impulses.

Ethical Behavior and Mindfulness

Mindfulness practice has shown to not only enhance ethical

awareness but also to influence behavior in ethical contexts. Research has indicated that mindfulness can lead to:

- A reduction in unethical decision-making.
- Enhanced empathy and compassion, leading to more pro-social behavior.
- Decreased aggression and reduced likelihood of engaging in harmful behavior.

The incorporation of mindfulness into ethical training programs in various professional fields, such as medicine, law, and business, further underscores its role in shaping ethical behavior.

Mindfulness: An Ethical Compass?

As we wade through the murky waters of ethical dilemmas, mindfulness can serve as a compass, providing a clearer sense of direction. It does not provide explicit ethical instructions but rather enhances our ability to engage with ethical questions in a more profound and nuanced manner. The practice of mindfulness, with its emphasis on non-judgmental awareness, presents a unique approach to ethics—one that is deeply introspective and personal, yet universally resonant in its quest for a more ethical existence.

Summary

This chapter has ventured into the interplay between mindfulness and meta-ethics, examining how mindfulness influences our understanding and practice of ethics. It has highlighted the ways in which mindfulness can enhance ethical awareness, influence meta-ethical positions, and shape ethical behavior. Mindfulness emerges not only as a tool for personal growth and emotional regulation but also as a significant factor in the realm of ethical philosophy and practice.

CHAPTER 39: QUANTUM CONSCIOUSNESS AND MINDFULNESS

The penultimate chapter of "Noetic Scrying: Divining Through Cognitive States" thrusts us into the compelling intersection of quantum consciousness and mindfulness. Here, we delve into the advanced theories positing connections between the quantum realm and the states of human consciousness enhanced through mindfulness. This chapter not only demystifies the complexities surrounding quantum mechanics but also delineates the potential interplay between this enigmatic domain and the practices of mindfulness and meditation.

Quantum Consciousness: A Primer Quantum consciousness is a term that invokes both intrigue and skepticism. Rooted in the principles of quantum mechanics, it suggests that consciousness emerges from the quantum level—a layer of reality that is fundamentally different from the macroscopic world we inhabit. Quantum mechanics, with its dual nature of particles and waves, superposition, and entanglement, has perplexed and fascinated scientists for over a century. Now, the question arises: could these principles be intricately woven into the tapestry of human consciousness?

At the heart of this conundrum lies the "quantum mind" hypothesis, which postulates that the brain operates at a quantum level. Proponents argue that quantum phenomena, like superposition and entanglement, could underlie cognitive functions and consciousness. However, this remains a contentious hypothesis within the scientific community, as definitive proof remains elusive.

Mindfulness and the Quantum Landscape The practice of mindfulness—rooted in focused attention, awareness of the present moment, and acceptance—might appear distant from the cold, mathematical realm of quantum mechanics. Yet, intriguing parallels emerge upon closer inspection. Mindfulness, at its core, is about transcending the ordinary, accessing deeper layers of awareness, and tapping into a profound sense of connectedness with the universe. Quantum mechanics, too, speaks of a reality beyond our usual sensory experiences, hinting at a level of connectedness that transcends time and space.

Advanced meditators often report experiences that echo quantum phenomena: a sense of unity with the environment (akin to quantum entanglement), an awareness of the simultaneous existence of multiple possibilities (reminiscent of superposition), and profound shifts in perception and reality. Could it be that through deep meditation and mindfulness practices, individuals are accessing a quantum level of consciousness?

Intersecting Paths: Quantum Consciousness in Mindfulness Practice The convergence of quantum consciousness and mindfulness practice might offer profound insights into the nature of reality and our place within it. Consider the concept of "observer effect" in quantum mechanics, which posits that the act of observation affects the state of what is being observed. Mindfulness, too, emphasizes the power of observation, encouraging practitioners to observe their thoughts and emotions non-judgmentally. In both instances, the act of observation becomes transformative.

Additionally, the concept of non-locality in quantum mechanics, where particles remain connected across vast distances, mirrors the sense of interconnectedness fostered through mindfulness practices. This interconnectedness speaks to a deeper level of consciousness, a unifying field that transcends physical separation.

Critiques and Controversies Despite the fascinating parallels, the intersection of quantum consciousness and mindfulness is not without its critics. The scientific community urges caution, emphasizing that while quantum mechanics is well-established in the realm of the very small (atoms and subatomic particles), its application to brain function and consciousness is speculative at best. Critics argue that the warm, wet, and noisy environment of the brain is unsuitable for delicate quantum states, which typically require extreme cold and isolation.

Moreover, there is a tendency to oversimplify and misrepresent quantum mechanics, leading to pseudoscientific claims. It is crucial to approach this intersection with both an open mind and a critical eye, seeking empirical evidence and robust theoretical frameworks.

In Conclusion As we traverse the complex landscape of quantum consciousness and mindfulness, it is clear that we are venturing into uncharted territories. While definitive answers may be elusive, the exploration itself is a testament to the human spirit's insatiable curiosity. Whether or not quantum mechanics and mindfulness are inextricably linked remains a subject of debate and investigation. What is undeniable, however, is the transformative power of mindfulness practices in deepening our understanding of ourselves and the cosmos. As we continue to probe the mysteries of the quantum world and the depths of human consciousness, we embark on a journey that has the potential to redefine our perception of reality itself.

CHAPTER 40: THE SHADOW SELF AND MINDFULNESS

Mindfulness, as an inward-facing journey, often reveals not only the placid lakes and verdant terrains of the mind but also its shadowy caverns and obscured crevices. In this chapter, we delve into the Jungian conception of the "Shadow Self," a critical component in advanced mindfulness practices, which entails recognizing and integrating the darker, often unacknowledged facets of our psyche.

The Shadow Self: Unveiling the Unconscious

Coined by the Swiss psychiatrist Carl Jung, the "Shadow Self" represents the parts of ourselves that we tend to hide, repress, or deny—traits, desires, and impulses that do not align with our ideal self-image. Jung posited that these repressed elements, while invisible to the conscious mind, influence behaviors and emotional responses. Mindfulness becomes a tool for unmasking the shadow, allowing practitioners to confront these hidden aspects without judgment, thereby initiating a process of deep psychological transformation.

Mindfulness and Shadow Work

Shadow work in mindfulness is not a trivial endeavor; it is an exploration that requires courage, honesty, and a willingness to face discomfort. Mindfulness practices provide a structured and compassionate space for this exploration. Meditation, for instance, fosters a heightened state of awareness and presence, where one can observe thoughts and emotions without immediate identification or reaction. Through consistent practice, it becomes possible to recognize patterns that may be indicative of the shadow, such as recurring negative thoughts, irrational fears, or inexplicable emotional responses.

Integration and Wholeness

The ultimate goal of engaging with the shadow through mindfulness is not to eradicate these darker aspects, for they are an integral part of the human experience. Rather, it is about integration—bringing these elements into conscious awareness and accepting them as components of our complete self. This integrative process promotes psychological wholeness and authenticity, as we cease to expend energy suppressing parts of ourselves. Additionally, it fosters a deeper understanding of our triggers and behavioral tendencies, leading to healthier coping mechanisms and interpersonal dynamics.

In summary, the exploration of the Shadow Self through mindfulness is a profound journey toward self-discovery and authenticity. It necessitates a deep dive into the often-avoided recesses of the mind, bringing to light the repressed and denied aspects of our being. Through mindful practices and reflection, we can integrate these elements, paving the way for psychological wholeness and a more genuine engagement with ourselves and the world around us. This chapter has delved into the intricate dance of light and shadow within the mind's landscape, underscoring mindfulness not only as a tool for relaxation but also as a key to unlocking the full spectrum of the human psyche.

CHAPTER 41: MINDFULNESS AND THE MULTIVERSE

A Multidimensional Mind

The concept of a multiverse proposes the existence of multiple universes coexisting alongside our own, a theory that stretches the limits of human cognition and confronts us with profound existential questions. Mindfulness, a practice rooted in present-moment awareness and non-judgmental observation, might seem antithetical to such a speculative and seemingly esoteric subject. Yet, this chapter delves into the intriguing intersection of mindfulness and the multiverse theory, exploring how cultivating a mindful state can enhance our understanding of these expansive concepts and potentially transform our experience of reality.

Mindfulness as a Cosmic Lens

Mindfulness, in its essence, is an exercise in expanding awareness, sharpening perception, and cultivating a deeper connection with the immediate experience. The practice entails a conscious disentanglement from the habitual patterns of thought and a steady focus on the unfolding present. This framework of heightened awareness parallels the intellectual openness required to contemplate the multiverse theory. Just as mindfulness encourages practitioners to embrace the boundless nature of the present moment, considering the multiverse invites an acknowledgement of the boundless nature of reality itself.

The multiverse theory suggests that our universe is but one of an infinite array of universes, each with its own distinct laws of physics, timelines, and possibly even versions of ourselves. Contemplating such a vast landscape naturally induces a sense of cognitive dissonance, challenging the mind to reconcile its accustomed perception of a singular, linear reality with the idea of infinite realities. Mindfulness equips individuals with the cognitive flexibility to navigate this dissonance, fostering a mental environment where seemingly paradoxical concepts can coexist without conflict.

Navigating Parallel Realities Through Mindfulness

The integration of mindfulness into the exploration of the multiverse theory is not merely philosophical; it has practical implications as well. For instance, a mindful approach to this theory can enhance cognitive elasticity, allowing individuals to entertain complex, multidimensional ideas without becoming cognitively overwhelmed. Moreover, mindfulness can serve as a grounding tool, anchoring individuals in a stable sense of self even as they ponder the existence of their countless other selves scattered across different universes.

Furthermore, the multiverse theory has the potential to radically shift our understanding of identity and existence. If countless versions of ourselves exist in parallel universes, what does this imply about the nature of the self? Mindfulness, with its emphasis on observing thoughts and emotions without attachment, provides a framework for exploring these questions without succumbing to existential angst. By maintaining a mindful stance, individuals can engage with these profound questions from a place of curiosity and openness rather than fear or confusion.

Mindfulness and the Multiverse: A Synergy of Exploration

In conclusion, the synergy between mindfulness and the multiverse theory offers a fascinating domain of exploration. Mindfulness, as a practice of expansive awareness and non-judgmental observation, provides a robust framework for contemplating the vast and complex notion of multiple universes. It equips individuals with the cognitive tools necessary to navigate the intellectual and existential challenges posed by the multiverse theory. In doing so, mindfulness not only enriches our understanding of the cosmos but also deepens our engagement with the immediate experience, reminding us of the boundless nature of both reality and the mind.

CHAPTER 42: ADVANCED MIND-MAPPING TECHNIQUES

Embarking on a journey into the deeper recesses of the mind, this chapter delves into the advanced mind-mapping techniques that serve as powerful tools for introspection and mindfulness. The art of mind-mapping, often associated with brainstorming and idea organization, transcends its utilitarian roots to become a profound exercise in noetic scrying. This chapter unveils the intricate processes that allow one to navigate the labyrinthine corridors of the psyche, forging pathways to untapped reservoirs of cognition and consciousness.

Cognitive Cartography: Mapping the Mind's Terrain

Cognitive cartography, a term we coin here, is the art of meticulously mapping the thought processes, emotions, memories, and insights that dwell within the mind. Unlike traditional mind-maps, which may simply outline topics or ideas, cognitive cartography demands a nuanced understanding of the mind's complex interrelations and subtleties. It is akin to drafting a topographical map of a landscape, accounting for the peaks and valleys of emotional experiences, the rivers of thought that flow ceaselessly, and the cavernous depths of subconscious insights.

To engage in cognitive cartography, one begins with a central concept or emotional state and allows the mind to freely associate, branching out in myriad directions. Each branch, however, is not merely a word or phrase but a narrative, a story that carries the emotional weight and cognitive significance of the experience or thought it represents. Through this process, one uncovers the layered interconnections between seemingly disparate aspects of their psyche, revealing patterns and insights that might otherwise remain obscured.

Dialectical Synthesis: Harmonizing Dichotomies

Advanced mind-mapping techniques embrace the principle of dialectical synthesis—the reconciliation of opposites. In the context of noetic scrying, this involves identifying and exploring the polarities within one's thoughts and emotions. By plotting these dichotomies on a mind map, one initiates a dialogue between the contrasting elements. Through mindfulness, one observes the interplay of these forces, seeking a synthesis that transcends the initial opposition.

For instance, one might map the interrelation between fear and courage, passivity and action, or scarcity and abundance. By mindfully engaging with these dialectical pairs, one uncovers deeper truths about their cognitive and emotional landscapes, paving the way for a more harmonious and integrated self-understanding.

Metacognitive Mastery: The Observer Self

Incorporating metacognition—thinking about thinking—into mind-mapping techniques elevates the practice to new heights. By adopting the perspective of the observer self, one becomes a cartographer of their cognitive processes, tracing the pathways of thought with detached curiosity. This metacognitive mastery enables one to not only map their current cognitive state but also to anticipate and navigate future mental terrains.

Through this heightened awareness, the mind-mapper can identify cognitive patterns, such as repetitive thoughts or limiting beliefs, and plot alternative routes to foster more constructive and empowering thought processes. The metacognitive lens also allows for the identification of cognitive biases, enabling one to adjust their maps to reflect a more balanced and accurate representation of their inner world.

In conclusion, advanced mind-mapping techniques offer profound opportunities for introspection and mindfulness. By engaging in cognitive cartography, dialectical synthesis, and metacognitive mastery, one can traverse the rich and varied landscapes of the mind, uncovering insights and fostering a deeper connection with the self. This chapter serves as a guide to navigating the intricate networks of cognition and consciousness, providing tools for those who seek to chart their inner worlds with clarity and insight.

CHAPTER 43: MINDFULNESS AND COSMIC UNITY

In the intricate tapestry of mindfulness, the threads of individual existence intertwine with the grand fabric of the cosmos, painting a picture of profound interconnectedness. This chapter ventures into the advanced realms of mindfulness, exploring the profound concept of cosmic unity—an understanding that transcends the confines of the self and embraces the totality of existence. We delve into the essence of this interconnectedness, elucidating how mindfulness practices can guide us toward a recognition of our place within the cosmic order and foster a deep sense of unity with all that is.

The Fabric of Interconnectedness

At the heart of cosmic unity lies the realization that our existence is not isolated but is inextricably linked to the universe at large. This understanding is not just philosophical but is grounded in the tangible reality of our existence. Modern physics, particularly quantum mechanics, hints at an underlying field of energy that connects all things. This notion resonates with ancient wisdom traditions that have long espoused the belief in a fundamental interconnectedness permeating the cosmos.

Mindfulness, as a practice, can be a conduit to experiencing this interconnectedness. By cultivating a heightened awareness of the present moment and dissolving the barriers of ego, one can begin to sense the fabric of interconnectedness. Such experiences are often described as moments of profound insight or enlightenment, where the practitioner feels at one with the universe.

Dissolving the Illusion of Separateness

The sense of separation that we typically experience is largely a construct of the mind, reinforced by societal norms and personal beliefs. Mindfulness challenges this illusion by encouraging us to observe our thoughts, sensations, and emotions without attachment. As we become more adept at observing the transient nature of our experiences, the solidity of the ego begins to soften, revealing the fluidity of our existence.

This dissolution of separateness is not about losing one's identity but rather understanding that our true essence is not confined to the narrow parameters of the ego. It is about recognizing that our consciousness is a drop in the vast ocean of cosmic consciousness.

Practices to Experience Cosmic Unity

The journey toward experiencing cosmic unity through mindfulness is both personal and profound. It involves a range of practices that guide practitioners beyond the surface level of awareness. Advanced meditation techniques, such as deep contemplative meditation or Dzogchen, aim to bring about a non-dual awareness where the distinction between the observer and the observed diminishes.

Another powerful practice is the 'Metta Bhavana' or loving-kindness meditation. This practice involves the cultivation of unconditional love and compassion, not only towards oneself and others but also towards all beings. As this love expands, the artificial boundaries between self and other begin to dissolve, paving the way for a heartfelt experience of unity.

Nature immersion is yet another pathway to experiencing cosmic unity. Spending time in natural settings, observing the intricate patterns of life, and realizing our part in the grand scheme of things can evoke a sense of oneness with the cosmos.

The Transformative Impact of Cosmic Unity

Experiencing cosmic unity through mindfulness can be transformative. It can shift our perspective from a self-centric view to a more holistic understanding of our place in the universe. This shift can have profound implications for how we live our lives. It can foster a deeper sense of compassion, empathy, and a sense of responsibility towards the planet and all its inhabitants.

Moreover, this understanding can be a source of immense peace and solace. Knowing that we are part of something much larger can provide comfort in times of isolation or despair. It can also serve as a powerful motivator for personal and collective growth, inspiring us to live in harmony with each other and the natural world.

In conclusion, the journey towards cosmic unity is a profound aspect of advanced mindfulness practices. It involves transcending the illusion of separateness, embracing the interconnectedness of all existence, and realizing our integral part in the cosmic dance. As we embark on this journey, we open ourselves to transformative experiences that can enrich our lives and elevate our consciousness. Through mindful exploration, we discover not just the universe's vastness, but also the boundless potential within ourselves to connect with it in a deep and meaningful way.

CHAPTER 44: NOETIC SCRYING IN MYSTICAL TRADITIONS

In the labyrinthine corridors of mystical traditions, noetic scrying serves as a bridge between the mundane and the sublime, a portal through which practitioners traverse in pursuit of profound insights and heightened states of consciousness. This chapter delves into the intricate tapestry of mindfulness and meditation as they intertwine with various mystical traditions, revealing the shared threads and unique patterns that have enriched the tapestry of human spiritual pursuit.

Mindfulness in the Sufi Tradition

The Sufi tradition, known for its poetic expression and profound mysticism, presents a nuanced perspective on mindfulness. In Sufism, the practice of "Muraqaba," akin to meditation, involves vigilant self-observation and a focused awareness of the Divine Presence. Sufis aspire to a state of "Fana," where the self dissolves into the universal, a concept that echoes the oneness espoused in advanced mindfulness practices. This annihilation of the ego, or "Nafs," mirrors the objectives of noetic scrying, where practitioners seek to transcend their limited sense of self to access a more expansive state of being.

Zen Buddhism: The Art of Zazen

Zen Buddhism, with its emphasis on simplicity and direct experience, approaches mindfulness through "Zazen," or seated meditation. This practice encourages a non-dualistic awareness, where the meditator is neither attached to nor detached from their thoughts and sensations. Zen's approach to noetic scrying is not to seek answers but to immerse oneself deeply in the question, in the immediate experience, embodying the essence of the famous Zen koan, "What is the sound of one hand clapping?" The enigmatic nature of Zen practice fosters an advanced form of mindfulness that transcends conventional cognition.

Kabbalistic Meditation and the Tree of Life

In the mystical tradition of Kabbalah, meditation and contemplation revolve around the esoteric symbol of the Tree of Life, representing the emanations and attributes of the Divine. Kabbalistic practices often involve visualizations and the chanting of divine names, intended to align the practitioner with higher spiritual states. This form of noetic scrying is a quest for Divine wisdom, or "Da'at," a knowledge that transcends intellectual understanding. The mindfulness experienced through Kabbalistic meditation is one of active engagement with the hidden dimensions of reality, an intricate dance between the known and the unknowable.

Shamanic Journeying and Mindful Trance

Shamanism, an ancient spiritual tradition found in various cultures around the world, employs trance states and spirit journeys to access deeper realms of consciousness. These shamanic practices resonate with the concept of noetic scrying, where mindfulness is not a passive observation but an active exploration of other worlds and states of being. The shaman's drumbeat, akin to a mantra, serves as a vehicle for the practitioner to journey into the spiritual landscape, seeking insights and healing. This form of mindfulness is dynamic and interactive, involving a symbiotic relationship between the practitioner and the cosmos.

Conclusion

In exploring the role of noetic scrying in mystical traditions, we find a common thread—the pursuit of a deeper, more profound connection with the self, the divine, and the cosmos. Each tradition offers a unique lens through which mindfulness and meditation are not merely practices but gateways to transcendent experiences. The rich tapestry of these traditions provides a broader context for understanding noetic scrying, revealing it as a multifaceted gem whose brilliance is reflected in the diversity of human spiritual inquiry. As we continue our exploration, we carry with us the wisdom gleaned from these mystical paths, enriching our own practice of noetic scrying with the depth and nuance they offer.

CHAPTER 45: MINDFULNESS IN VIRTUAL REALITY

As we delve deeper into the labyrinthine corridors of human cognition and its myriad expressions, we encounter the juxtaposition of mindfulness with an ostensibly incongruent counterpart—virtual reality (VR). The convergence of these two realms may appear, at first glance, to be a paradoxical synthesis; however, a closer examination reveals a symbiotic relationship that enriches our understanding of mindfulness and extends its frontiers in unprecedented ways.

Transcending Traditional Boundaries

Virtual reality, in its essence, is a technological simulacrum, a fabricated digital cosmos meticulously crafted to emulate or surpass the phenomenological experience of reality. This digital alchemy offers an expansive palette for the exploration and expression of mindfulness. VR environments can be tailored to evoke specific cognitive and emotional responses, creating a controlled setting in which mindfulness can be cultivated and its effects meticulously observed.

The utilitarian aspect of VR in mindfulness lies in its capacity to simulate scenarios that might be logistically impractical or inaccessible in the physical world. Imagine, for instance, the replication of a tranquil Zen garden, complete with the murmuring of a meandering brook and the whispering of leaves stirred by an unseen breeze. Such serene vistas, once the privilege of the few, are now accessible to many through the medium of VR.

Enhanced Mindfulness Training

Virtual reality's immersive nature provides a potent catalyst for mindfulness training. It can engender a heightened sense of presence, the cornerstone of mindfulness, by diminishing the distractions of the external world and directing attention inward. The ability to create bespoke environments means that practitioners can be exposed to situations tailored to their individual needs or stages of mindfulness practice. From serene landscapes to complex, thought-provoking scenarios, VR offers a versatile canvas for mindfulness exploration.

Moreover, VR can serve as a valuable educational tool. Through interactive simulations, it can elucidate complex concepts related to mindfulness, such as the fluidity of perception or the illusory nature of the self, in a manner that is both engaging and experiential. This tangible approach to learning caters well to the contemporary zeitgeist, which often favors experiential knowledge over didactic instruction.

Research and Therapeutic Applications

The intersection of mindfulness and VR also holds promise in the domains of psychological research and therapy. By creating controlled and replicable environments, researchers can study the effects of mindfulness practices with greater precision. This can deepen our understanding of how mindfulness operates on a neurological level, potentially leading to the development of more effective mindfulness-based interventions.

In therapeutic settings, VR can serve as a powerful adjunct to mindfulness training. For individuals grappling with anxiety, phobias, or PTSD, VR can provide a safe space to confront and process their experiences. The controlled nature of VR allows for gradual exposure to triggering stimuli, while mindfulness techniques can be employed to navigate these experiences with greater equanimity and awareness.

Challenges and Considerations

Yet, the integration of VR into mindfulness practice is not without its challenges. The reliance on technology, which is often seen as antithetical to the spirit of mindfulness, raises questions about authenticity and dependence. Moreover, the immersive nature of VR can lead to escapism, where individuals might prefer the simulated worlds over the reality of their present moment, paradoxically undermining the very essence of mindfulness.

Thus, the incorporation of VR into mindfulness practice must be approached with discernment. It should be seen not as a replacement for traditional practices but as a complementary tool that offers new dimensions and possibilities. The efficacy of VR in mindfulness hinges on its judicious use, ensuring that it enhances rather than detracts from the mindfulness experience.

Concluding Reflections

In the penultimate chapter of our exploration, the confluence of mindfulness and virtual reality symbolizes the evolving landscape of human cognition and the innovative ways in which we seek to understand and enhance it. Mindfulness in virtual reality is not just a testament to our technological prowess but also a reflection of our perennial quest to transcend the boundaries of our consciousness. As we stand on the precipice of these new horizons, we are reminded of the limitless potential of the human mind and the myriad paths that lie before us in our quest for understanding, balance, and inner tranquility.

CHAPTER 46: EXISTENTIALISM AND MINDFULNESS

Existentialism, a philosophical movement that arose in the 19th and 20th centuries, concerns itself with the human condition, focusing on concepts such as freedom, choice, and the search for meaning amidst an inherently meaningless universe. It posits that individuals are free and responsible agents determining their own development through acts of will. This chapter delves into the profound connections between existentialism and mindfulness, exploring how these seemingly disparate realms intersect and enhance each other, providing a nuanced understanding of existence and consciousness.

Existential Awareness and Present Moment Consciousness: Mindfulness, the practice of being fully present and engaged in the moment, free from distraction or judgment, aligns closely with existentialist philosophy. The convergence is evident in the shared emphasis on individual experience and autonomy. Mindfulness amplifies existential awareness, allowing one to confront the fundamental truths of existence—such as freedom, isolation, and mortality—with a clear and focused mind. This heightened awareness engenders a profound sense of being truly alive, acutely aware of one's own existence and the choices that mold it.

Freedom, Responsibility, and Mindful Choice: Existentialism

asserts that with freedom comes immense responsibility. Every action, every decision, is a testament to one's freedom, and thus, each individual must bear the weight of their choices. Mindfulness complements this notion by fostering a heightened sense of awareness and attentiveness, enabling individuals to make more deliberate and conscious choices. Through the lens of mindfulness, one recognizes the breadth of their freedom and the consequential nature of their actions, cultivating a sense of responsibility that is deeply rooted in the present moment.

The Absurd and the Search for Meaning: Existentialism posits that the universe is fundamentally devoid of meaning, a concept known as "the Absurd." This realization often leads to existential angst, a profound sense of disorientation and confusion in the face of an apparently meaningless or absurd world. Mindfulness, by anchoring individuals in the present moment, offers a potent antidote to this existential despair. It provides a way to navigate the Absurd, not by seeking to impose meaning where there is none, but by finding peace and contentment in the mere act of being. In the mindful state, one learns to appreciate the intrinsic value of each moment, regardless of the overarching narrative of one's life.

Confronting Existential Angst with Mindful Acceptance: Existential angst can manifest as a pervasive sense of dread or anxiety stemming from the contemplation of life's ultimate concerns, such as death, freedom, isolation, and meaninglessness. Mindfulness practices encourage a non-judgmental acceptance of one's thoughts and feelings, which can be particularly therapeutic when grappling with these existential concerns. By observing these thoughts without attachment, individuals learn to coexist with existential angst, understanding it as a natural component of the human experience rather than an adversary to be vanquished.

Authentic Existence and Mindful Living: The concept of "authenticity" is central to existentialism, denoting a way of life in which one is true to their own personality, spirit, or character, despite external pressures. Mindfulness nurtures authenticity by stripping away the layers of social conditioning and habitual reaction, revealing the raw, unadulterated self. It encourages living authentically, not as a byproduct of external validation or societal expectations, but as a reflection of one's true desires and values. Mindful living, therefore, is an existential pursuit, a journey towards a life lived genuinely and purposefully.

In summary, existentialism and mindfulness, though originating from distinct philosophical and cultural backgrounds, share a profound kinship. Both realms advocate for a deeply personal engagement with existence, encouraging individuals to confront the inherent complexities of life with openness, awareness, and authenticity. Through the practice of mindfulness, the existential journey becomes not a burdensome odyssey through a meaningless landscape but a vibrant dance with existence itself, one that celebrates freedom, embraces responsibility, and finds solace in the beauty of the present moment.

CHAPTER 47: MINDFULNESS AND EPIGENETICS

As our journey through the profound and multifaceted world of mindfulness reaches its zenith, we delve into the intricate interplay between mindfulness and the burgeoning field of epigenetics. This chapter invites readers to transcend the boundaries of the mind and body, to explore how the ancient practice of mindfulness can exert influence at the molecular level, potentially orchestrating changes in gene expression.

The Confluence of Mind and Gene

The advent of epigenetics has revolutionized our understanding of genetics, revealing that our DNA is not the immutable blueprint it was once thought to be. Epigenetics, a term coined by merging 'epi' (Greek for 'over, outside of, around') with 'genetics', explores the dynamic modifications that influence gene expression without altering the DNA sequence. These modifications can be likened to a complex symphony, where the notes—the DNA sequence—remain constant, but the expression and intensity—epigenetic markers—fluctuate, conducted by environmental cues.

Mindfulness, a practice rooted in ancient traditions and refined through contemporary psychological discourse, has emerged as a fascinating conductor in this symphonic interplay. Mindfulness practices, through their emphasis on sustained, non-judgmental awareness, have been shown to modulate physiological stress responses. This modulation is not merely a transient alteration in subjective experience but extends its tendrils to the epigenetic level, influencing the way genes are expressed.

Epigenetic Markers: The Language of Interaction

To comprehend the dialogue between mindfulness and epigenetics, it is imperative to acquaint ourselves with the primary mechanisms of epigenetic modification. Among these, DNA methylation and histone modification stand out as critical processes. DNA methylation involves the addition of a methyl group to the DNA molecule, often resulting in gene silencing. Histone modification, on the other hand, alters the packaging of DNA, thereby modulating gene accessibility and expression.

Emerging research in the realm of psychoneuroimmunology has shed light on how stress and emotion regulation, pivotal elements in mindfulness practices, can influence these epigenetic mechanisms. For instance, mindfulness-based interventions have been correlated with decreased DNA methylation levels in genes associated with inflammatory responses. This suggests a potential pathway through which mindfulness could mitigate chronic inflammation, a known contributor to a plethora of diseases.

Gene Expression: A Dance with Mindfulness

One of the most compelling arenas where mindfulness and epigenetics intersect is in the domain of mental health. Psychological distress and disorders are complex tapestries woven from threads of genetic predispositions, environmental factors, and personal experiences. Mindfulness practices, by engendering a heightened state of awareness and emotional regulation, can influence this tapestry at the genetic level.

For example, individuals engaging in regular mindfulness meditation have demonstrated alterations in gene expression profiles associated with improved stress response, reduced inflammation, and enhanced cellular repair mechanisms. These changes not only underscore the profound impact of mindfulness on well-being but also highlight its potential role in altering the trajectory of mental health disorders.

Future Horizons: Mindfulness as an Epigenetic Modulator

As we stand on the precipice of this burgeoning field, the horizon is alight with possibilities. The synthesis of mindfulness and epigenetics beckons a future where personalized medicine could integrate these practices to optimize health outcomes. Imagine a scenario where mindfulness interventions are prescribed, not just for their psychological benefits, but for their capacity to modulate gene expression in a targeted manner, akin to a precision-guided epigenetic therapy.

Moreover, the implications of this confluence extend beyond individual health, gesturing toward transgenerational effects. The epigenetic modifications induced by mindfulness could potentially be passed down, offering a transformative tool for breaking cycles of trauma and predisposition to certain illnesses.

As we approach the culmination of our exploration, it is clear that the intersection of mindfulness and epigenetics is a frontier teeming with potential. It challenges us to reconceptualize the boundaries between mind and body, between subjective experience and molecular biology. This chapter has illuminated a path where mindfulness is not merely a practice for mental tranquility but a key that unlocks profound biological transformations. As we harness the power of mindfulness to shape our genetic destiny, we are reminded of the remarkable plasticity and resilience inherent in the tapestry of life.

CHAPTER 48: A FRIENDLY, POSITIVE CONCLUSION

As we arrive at the final leg of our odyssey through the landscapes of consciousness, mindfulness, and meditation, it's essential to cast a gentle, retrospective glance over the terrain we've traversed. From the rudimentary understanding of mindfulness and its foundational practices to the intricate interplay of cognitive states and their potential to divine deeper insights, we've embraced a rich tapestry of knowledge, experiences, and wisdom.

Reflecting on the Journey

Our journey commenced with an accessible foray into the realms of noetic scrying—a blend of intuition, consciousness, and the profound power of mindfulness and meditation. We embarked on this path with an open heart, curious mind, and a sense of wonder, exploring the rudimentary aspects of mindfulness in our initial chapters. From the first breaths of mindful awareness to the foundational practices that bring us into the present moment, we unlocked the gateway to a more attentive existence.

As we progressed, our exploration deepened, delving into the intermediate concepts and practices. We touched upon the transformative power of mindfulness on our neural landscapes, the ethereal qualities of transcendental meditation, and the integration of mindfulness into our daily routines and relationships. Each chapter served as a stepping stone, leading us to an enhanced understanding and a more profound appreciation of our cognitive and emotional selves.

Advanced Insights and Revelations

The advanced chapters unveiled a new horizon, where the esoteric, scientific, and philosophical converged. Here, we untangled the complex threads of quantum consciousness, navigated the mysterious terrains of the multiverse, and contemplated the profound implications of mindfulness on our genetic tapestry. These chapters were not merely informative but transformative, inviting us to expand our perceptions of reality, consciousness, and the self.

Integrating Wisdom into Daily Life

As we close this chapter and reflect on the insights gleaned, it's paramount to consider how we can integrate this wisdom into our daily lives. Mindfulness is not merely a practice but a way of being—a continuous dance of awareness and presence that enriches every moment, interaction, and experience. The techniques and philosophies we've encountered are tools, but their true value emerges when we weave them into the fabric of our everyday existence.

Embracing the Continuous Journey

Mindfulness and meditation are not destinations but journeys —ones without a definitive endpoint. Each breath, each mindful moment, each meditative practice is a step forward on an endless path of discovery and growth. As we integrate the lessons from this book into our lives, we may find that mindfulness becomes a cherished companion, guiding us through the vicissitudes of life with grace, resilience, and a profound sense of interconnectedness.

In the end, noetic scrying is about peering inward to the depths of our being and outward to the vastness of the cosmos with the same curious gaze, recognizing that the microcosm of our inner world reflects the macrocosm of the universe. It's a journey of unity, where the scryer and the scryed are one, and the act of divination becomes a dance of consciousness with the rhythms of existence.

With this friendly, positive conclusion, we part ways, but the journey continues. May the wisdom of mindfulness and meditation illuminate your path, and may your journey through cognitive states be filled with wonder, insight, and profound revelations.

THE END

Printed in Great Britain
by Amazon